A Future Economy for All

Mohamed Rabie

A Future Economy for All

Creating a Free, Just, and Sustainable Economic Future

palgrave
macmillan

Mohamed Rabie
Arab Thought Council
Washington, DC, USA

ISBN 978-3-031-42956-9 ISBN 978-3-031-42957-6 (eBook)
https://doi.org/10.1007/978-3-031-42957-6

This Palgrave Macmillan imprint is published by the registered company Springer Nature Switzerland AG
The registered company address is: Gewerbestrasse 11, 6330 Cham, Switzerland

Paper in this product is recyclable.

Contents

About the Author

Prof. Mohamed Rabie is a distinguished professor of International Political Economy; he attended 5 universities and taught at 11 others on four continents. He has published 61 books, about 200 scholarly papers, and over 2000 newspaper articles. 16 books are in English, one in Albanian, and the rest are in Arabic. English books include 4 books published by Palgrave Macmillan. One of the English books, "History of Racism", was translated and published in six other languages: German, French, Italian, Spanish, Portuguese, and Polish. Arabic Books include 3 poetry collections, 3 novels, and a story; the rest is mostly academic books and collections of ideas and reflections. Prof. Rabie is president of the Arab Thought Council in Washington, DC, a member of the Arab Thought Forum, and a fellow of the Alexander Von Humboldt Foundation since 1992. Grants and scholarships financed his education from high school to receiving his Ph.D. in 1970 from the University of Houston; grants covered studies in Jordan, Egypt, Germany, and America. He is the winner of the State of Palestine Lifetime Achievement Award for scholarly publications and other awards. His writings and positions reflect a strong commitment to peace, social justice, freedom, human development, and social, cultural, economic, and environmental sustainability.

www.yazour.com

CHAPTER 1

Introduction

Abstract I believe that the world entered around the mid-1990s a transitional period that is taking us from the industrial age to the "knowledge age". Transitional periods are characterized by chaos and loss of direction that cause the major pillars of society to crumble, and most theories to lose their validity and become in need of restructuring. Meanwhile, the laws and regulations lose their capacity to deal with the emerging situation, causing a "trust deficit" to be created. This causes injustice to spread and the wealth and income gaps to widen. The book articulates proposals to restructure the system while emphasizing social justice and sustainability.

Keyword Sustainability · Trust deficit · Social justice · Knowledge

Our world of today can be described as a world in a continuous state of transition, where everything changes in front of our eyes, while we stand looking rather helpless, unable to control, change, or influence its direction. On the other hand, none of the old roadmaps, theories, or strategies is able to explain the nature of change or its destination, assuming that it has a destination. In fact, the pace of change seems to accelerate with every day passes and become multidimensional. In the meantime, racism, extremism, and discrimination, which had been on the decline for more

M. Rabie, *A Future Economy for All*,
https://doi.org/10.1007/978-3-031-42957-6_1

than half a century, have raised their ugly faces to take the initiative in the most politically, socially, and economically developed Western states, signaling that the human race is in deep trouble. In addition, ideological polarization in many major states, especially in America, has caused the democratic system to stop functioning properly and failed to provide the public services it is supposed to provide. As a result, the capacities of the ruling political elites in each state can no longer reach compromises to deal with the major pressing problems and challenges the world is facing today.

Although the West, led by the United States, continues to claim that it is entitled to lead the world, I believe that the West has never had a collective leadership that is politically and economically corrupt and morally and intellectually bankrupt as the one we have today; therefore it can neither lead nor has the moral authority to lead. In the meantime, public trust in the major organs of the state has declined, particularly in the United States, which makes the concept of representative government more of a fiction than a reality. While the rich are getting richer and the poor are getting poorer, business ethics has disappeared everywhere, allowing manipulation and cheating to take its place; and sometimes stealing whatever they can from the poor and the uninformed that need help most.

For a society to function properly and be stable and productive, it must have three major pillars: First, an efficient political system that gives every citizen a vote in the making of decisions that affect his life through his elected representatives. Second, it needs an efficient economic system that gives every citizen an equal opportunity to work and have access to the financial markets to borrow and meet emergencies and investment capital. Third, it needs efficient and just education and healthcare systems that provide all citizens with free quality education and free healthcare.

In addition, to have all these systems function properly and deliver the services they are meant to deliver, there is a need for a tax system that collects enough money to fund the three systems and ensure that the wealth and income gaps in every society are kept within reasonable bounds. This is needed to give everyone a chance to climb the social ladder without resorting to misconduct. However, "Racial, income, and wealth inequality have severely choked off intergenerational upward mobility during the last few decades. Inherited money and skin color are greater predictors of life success than hard work, intelligence, personal responsibility and discipline".[1]

Since the United States is the leader of the so-called Free World, any attempt to analyze the efficiency of the three pillars of Western society must focus on America. In fact, while Western Europe has had its own way of life for several decades, it is now following the United States' steps. And though many nations are trying to adopt the Western model, most Asian nations are moving in a different direction and developing new political and economic systems that defy the Western model. The future, therefore, is more likely to witness severe competition between the two models. I believe that the Western model is too weak to prevail in the long run; it needs deep social, economic, and political restructuring to have a chance of sharing the future.

Under the influence of the free market system, and because of the pressure applied by special interest groups on behalf of the rich and large corporations, the Western welfare state is in retreat. Social responsibility toward the poor, the elderly, and the community has lost its appeal. Consequently, poverty and the social ills associated with it such as crime, homelessness, drug use, ignorance, and racism have become endemic. In addition, consumerism and the inclination to borrow beyond one's ability to repay in order to satisfy one's desires have caused the average person in America and many Western countries to drown in debt and struggle to make ends meet; and that in turn is leading people to become apathetic, losing concern for other peoples and national and international issues; even interest in protecting the environment has lost some of its previous vigor.

This book will try to examine the status of the three major pillars of Western societies, identify their weaknesses, and provide suggestions to restructure them in ways that make them efficient, fair, and responsive to people's needs and able to deal with evolving knowledge age we live in today.

Notes

1. Chauncey DeVega, AlterNet.org, April 22, 2019.

CHAPTER 2

One Human Race; a Shared Destiny

Abstract This chapter tries to prove that all humans belong to one race only, the human race and have a shared destiny that can and should influence but cannot change.

Keywords Creation · Evolution · Darwinism · God · Religion · Adam · Eve · Color · Race · Nationality · Identity · Truth · Fiction

This is a narrative that tries to answer five basic questions concerning our existence and future as human beings living on earth, our only home. One; how did we get to be where we are and how are we doing today? Second, how should we understand the concepts of nation and nationality? Third, how should we view religion and its role in our lives? Four; how should we understand the meaning of the word "truth"? Five; who are our major adversaries? The arguments that follow are partially scientific, partially theological, and partially philosophical.

First, there are two major theories that try to explain how human beings became what they are today: the first is the creation theory, which claims that all humans were created by a mighty, mysterious power called God; the other is the evolutionary theory, developed by Charles Darwin, that claims that all creatures evolved from primitive species over billions of

M. Rabie, *A Future Economy for All*,
https://doi.org/10.1007/978-3-031-42957-6_2

years, starting about 4 billion years ago, and continued to evolve reaching what they are today.

People who believe in creation also believe that all humans are the descendants of one man (Adam) and one woman (Eve). Since we have the same mother and the same father, we must therefore be one people belonging to the same and only race, the human race. People who believe in evolution also believe that we all came from an animal that looks like an ape that appeared first in Africa hundreds of thousands of years ago; and from there people moved in bands to populate Mother Earth. So both theories say that all of us share a common ancestor and therefore we are one race. In fact, whenever we define ourselves, we tend to unconsciously say the human race, not the human races.

On our way to populate the earth, we were exposed to three powerful forces that shaped our life experiences and greatly influenced the way we look, live, think, and behave. These forces are: first, natural selection, or the law of the survival of the fittest, which caused some humans, animals, and plants to survive and flourish, and many more to perish. Second, random mutation gave us the many shades of black and white and yellow, and the diversified features we have today. Third, an unpredictable and often harsh environment forced us to move from one place to another and adapt to nature's dictates and its changing mood, which caused us to develop different cultures, many religions, countless languages, and forge unique associations with place and each other. Consequently, we gained cultural and religious diversity, but we encountered no other races on our way to where we are today to acquire racial diversity.

Embracing our cultural and religious diversity enriches our lives, opens our minds, and fills our hearts with joy. In contrast, believing in racial diversity poisons our hearts, closes our minds, undermines our shared sense of brotherhood, and leads us to hate one another, fight with each other, and damage our shared environment.

Second, nationality is a shared identity associated with a certain land and state; some nations have more in common than land and state, they have a shared language, culture, and/or history. A German, for example, is a person who was most likely born in Germany and identifies with the German land and state; Germans also share a language and a historical experience. An American is a person who lives in the United States and is a citizen of the USA; however, Americans have no shared history or culture. Indians, meanwhile, speak tens of languages and have hundreds of religions, yet they are one nation inhabiting the same land and having allegiance to the same state. In fact, if the United States, with its 330 million people coming from every place on earth carrying their traditions and religions can be called a nation, then any people sharing a land and belonging to one state must be considered a nation. Thus nationality is identification with a particular land and state only.

Third; Religion is an accident of birth; we all know that no one of us had the liberty to choose the religion he was born into. Today, as ever, no one can choose his parents, religion, place of birth, time of birth, his name, color, or social class at birth. Therefore, no one should be punished or rewarded because of things he inherited at birth: religion, identity, color, name, social class, or wealth; everyone should have the right to stay in his inherited religion, change it, or abandon it; and it is the duty of society to respect everyone's religious choice, and the responsibility of the state to protect everyone's religious and nonreligious rights.

People who believe in God also believe that religion and what comes with it at birth is an act of God. Since it is God who chooses for each one his parents and religion, place, and life conditions at birth, no believer is in a position to reject God's will. Nevertheless, most believers tend to accept God's will when it comes to their inherited religion and reject God's will when it comes to other people's religions. Since God chooses for each one of us his religion, every religion must be considered legitimate and thus must be respected by every believer; anyone who refuses to accept other peoples' religions is in fact rejecting the will of the God he claims to believe in and worship. No rational believer therefore can accept what God chooses for him and, at the same time, rejects what God chooses for his fellow human beings.

Fourth; how should we interpret the word "fact" or "truth"? Both words tend to refer to the same thing, and therefore the truth should be understood as something that at least one person in the world believes to be true or a fact. This thing could be an imagined one like the devil, or an incident that happened in the past like miracles, or a claim that embodies information that tells the story of an entity like a nation or religion. Nevertheless, every fact or truth that falls into one of these categories has three characteristics; it is relative; partial, and tentative. It is relative because some people believe it to be a fact and others do not; it is partial because everyone looking at it can see only one side of it; and it is tentative because science could prove it to be wrong.

For example, belief in miracles is relative because miracles defy human experience and because only some people believe they happened. A mountain that stands in front of our eyes is a partial fact because no one can see it in its entirety at one time. The truth is also tentative because it is subject to change due to natural and cultural and scientific factors. For example, until the seventeenth century most people in the world believed that earth was flat and the center of the universe, and that the sun rotates around it. Then science came to prove that the earth was oval, not flat, and represents a tiny portion of the universe, not its center; and it rotates around the sun and not the other way around.

Fifth; the most serious challenge that faces humanity today is the widening income and wealth gaps between the rich and poor. Income and wealth reports indicate that the richest 1% of the world's population owns over 50% of the world's wealth, which means that this 1% owns more than the rest 99% of the world's population whose number is about 8 billion. In fact, the richest 42 men in the world own as much wealth as the poorest 50% of the world's population, whose number exceeds 3.9 billion. Due to the tremendous power that the rich have, they can manipulate every system and situation and take advantage of every opportunity to enrich themselves and accumulate more wealth. In addition, reports indicate that the richest 10% of the world's population owns 85% of the world's wealth, leaving 15% to the other 90% of the people. Income reports indicate that about 95% of the annual increase in income goes to the richest 10% of the people, leaving 5% to the other 90%. This explains why the middle class is shrinking and losing power, and why poverty is spreading and becoming structural, causing alienation, radicalism, and racism to spread all over the world.

This means that the current global social order is unfair and needs to be reformed to protect the rights of the poor and weak. Though unfair orders are unsustainable in the long run, we should not wait for things to happen to us; we must make things happen for us, because no social order will change by itself. Therefore, we, the people, should take the initiative, articulate programs for change, and create social movements capable of effecting the desired change. This also means that our anger should not be directed at the rich but at the social order and ourselves because we failed to do our job in exposing the excesses of the system and opposing the policies that got us to this point. Since the rich work hard to perpetuate the current social order, we need to work harder to change it and liberate ourselves from the existing socioeconomic and sociopolitical orders that keep many of us weak and poor and undermine the future of future generations.

In addition, economic reports indicate that 50 of the world's largest 100 economies were corporations at the end of the twentieth century. In 2017 corporations represented 69 of the world's largest 100 economies; all such corporations are either owned or controlled by the richest 1% of the world's people. However, no two rich states or individuals are at war with each other, but many poor ones are fighting each other or involved in bloody and destructive civil wars. As we fight each other, we waste a good portion of our precious natural and human resources; in the meantime, the money we spend buying weapons and ammunition goes to enrich the rich, and further impoverish the poor. As a consequence, we remain poor and largely enslaved, killing each other instead of working with one another to liberate ourselves from poverty, need, and oppression and restore our sanity and humanity. In addition, "the 10 richest men in the world have seen their global wealth double to $1.5 trillion since the start of the global pandemic following a surge in share and property prices that has widened the gap between rich and poor, according to a report from Oxfam."[1]

To achieve our sociopolitical goals and reclaim a fair share of the world's wealth, we must realize that we, 90% of the world's population, share the same grievances, hopes, and destiny. Therefore, anyone who stands with a deprived minority somewhere is, unconsciously, standing against another deprived minority elsewhere. As we seek change, we need to further realize that neither the free market system nor the democratic system can by itself correct its mistakes and enable us to achieve our objectives; both systems have become largely dysfunctional. Therefore, we need to create a mass movement covering all parts of the world and articulate a strategy for change that seeks to transform the existing economic and political systems and replace them with a new global social order that guarantees fairness. Reclaiming our rights can only be achieved by working together in a peaceful manner to deny our adversaries any excuse to label us as radicals trying to destroy this or that culture and undermine peoples' ways of life in the West or East, North or South.

Being one and the same race, having traveled the same road, and driving to reach similar goals should make us, poor and rich, strong and weak, view each other as brothers, sisters, friends, lovers, and colleagues; embrace our shared humanity, celebrate our cultural and religious diversity, and learn from each other the art of living together in peace and harmony. Again, embracing our cultural and religious diversity enriches our lives; believing in racial diversity undermines our humanity.

Our motto should be *together, we empower each other, form a global power, create an economically, environmentally, and socially sustainable society, and change our world forever.*

Notes

1. https://www.theguardian.com/business/2022/jan/17/world-10-richest-men-see-their-wealth-double-during-covid-pandemic.

CHAPTER 3

Historical Background

Abstract This chapter tries to familiarize the reader of the historical transformations that humanity went through to reach the current situation, moving from the hunter-gatherer stage to the tribal stage, to the agricultural stage, to the industrial stage, and finally to the knowledge stage in which we are living today. It also explains the process of transformation and the forces that caused it.

Keywords Civilization · Culture · Globalization · Transformation · Historical discontinuity · Tribal · Agricultural · Industrial · Hamlets · Landlords · Slaves · Religion

On their way to the current age, human societies passed through three major stages of societal development or civilizations, with each stage causing all aspects of life to change fundamentally and irreversibly; change included society, economy, and culture, as well as social, economic, and political structures and production relations. Most historians and social scientists seem to acknowledge that the greatest revolutions in human history were the agricultural and industrial revolutions, which gave birth to the agricultural and industrial civilizations, respectively. Historians also agree that those two revolutions have had the greatest impact on people's life conditions and their perspective on life and the future. There is also an

M. Rabie, *A Future Economy for All*,
https://doi.org/10.1007/978-3-031-42957-6_3

agreement on at least three major stages of societal development: the pre-agricultural or the tribal stage, the agricultural stage, and the industrial stage.

Furthermore, a number of social thinkers believe that the information and communications revolutions of the 1990s represent another transformational change in our social history that is transforming the social, cultural, and economic conditions of life and how societies are organized. This new stage is often referred to as the information age, or the globalization age, or the digital age. However, I call it the *Knowledge Age* because it is knowledge that includes the information and telecommunications revolutions, and the recent technological innovations and scientific discoveries and ideas that launched the Knowledge Revolution in the mid-1990s. Analyzing these stages and how they relate to each other should enable us to place social, cultural, political, and economic changes in their proper historical and societal contexts and track the course of societal development over time, and thus understand where we came from, where we are now, and where we are expected to go.

Each stage of development had come after a difficult, oftentimes long transitional period; during which the major institutions, roadmaps, theories, and ideas of the old society lose their validity and ability to explain the changing life conditions and manage change. In fact, each transitional period represents a *historical discontinuity*, during which the history and historical logic and wisdom of the passing era come to an end; and this paves the way for the new era to chart its history and depict its particular logic. Since no one knows in such circumstances what lies ahead, chaos rather than order characterizes life conditions and causes the theories and institutions and grand ideas that had managed all aspects of life to start crumbling, while no new ones are developed in time to replace them. As chaos spreads and prevails, a general sense of loss of direction overwhelms society, causing people in charge of managing the many aspects of life to feel confused and disoriented. Nevertheless, at the end of each transitional period a new civilization emerges having its own society, culture, and economy; and this causes the old social and economic structures and production relations to change fundamentally.[1]

Historical discontinuities are unique developments that make people's experience similar to that of a driver entering an unfamiliar mountainous terrain. As the driver takes a long curve on a winding road, he loses sight of the familiar landscape that lies behind him, while the mountains he negotiates block his view, preventing him from seeing the landscape that lies ahead, causing his speed and control of the vehicle to become subject to the rough terrain. As a consequence, his expectations and confidence become subject to the ups and downs of the winding road. The familiar landscape that lies behind no longer helps; the horizon that looms in the sky is so vast and obscured it provides little clues to what lies ahead.[2]

Historical records of older times suggest that long before the development of agriculture human beings were able to get enough food and attain a sufficient level of security to survive and grow. Familial and tribal ties served as a social glue that held early societies together and gave meaning to their individual and communal lives. Members of each tribe behaved as if they were members of one family whose survival dictates cooperation and strict adherence to tribal traditions, customs, and norms. This means that the roots of civilization came into existence probably 20,000 years before the dawn of the agricultural age. However, it was a primitive civilization based on a food economy that depended primarily on hunting animals and collecting wild fruits and vegetables.

Nevertheless, about one thousand years before the development of agriculture, man was able to domesticate many animals and use them as means of transportation and sources of meat; man also used the skin, hair, and bones of some animals for other purposes. On the other hand, due to its nomadic life, the tribal society did not know the kind of injustice or alienation associated with social classes, which succeeding civilizations witnessed and endured until today and because the private property institution did not and could not exist in the tribal age due to its way of life, the tribal society was classless; it was made of only one social class. However, tribes fought each other for a reason and often for no reason at all. As a consequence, the **tribal man fought to live and lived to fight, making his life starts and ends with fighting.**

With the development of agriculture some 12,000 years ago, the economic base of society began to change fundamentally, causing the culture and social and economic structures of the tribal society to change in ways that made them different from the older ones. "Plant and animal domestication meant much more food and hence much denser human populations. The resulting food surpluses and the animal-based means of transporting the surpluses, were a prerequisite for the development of settled, politically centralized, socially stratified, economically complex, technologically innovative societies."[3] The development of agriculture changed the way societies and economies were organized and transformed peoples' cultures and their relationships to each other and to their environment. Agriculture brought about a new civilization having its own society, culture, economy, production relations, and social and political organization. "The change from hunting and gathering to agriculture involved more than a mere change in subsistence pattern; it represented a complete change in the social and cultural fabric of life; it meant also a mental change."[4]

As farming the land became indispensable to the survival of agricultural society, the private property institution emerged as a powerful force playing a transformational role in the social and economic relations in society. In the meantime, the appearance of scattered agricultural hamlets and villages necessitated the development of a superstructure, or a state to regulate the ownership of agricultural land and the sharing of water resources and to protect hamlets and villages from roaming tribesmen looking for people to victimize. Consequently, politically centralized, economically complex, and technologically innovative societies appeared slowly; causing the agricultural society to be divided into two social classes: landlords who were rich; and farmers and farm workers and slaves who were poor. Since wealth is a major source of power, landlords were able to forge alliances with the forces of the political process or the state and gain more power and influence at the expense of the small farmers, farm workers, and slaves.

The food surplus that the agricultural society produced enabled some people, particularly the rich, to have enough time to think and speculate about the past and future and life in general. This gave rise to religion and the sacred, causing human relations to change and tie believers to each other in addition to their families and clans. So before the state appeared as a superstructure, religion appeared as a social system and a source of knowledge that comforted the poor and the slaves and urged the rich to help the poor and the powerful to assist the weak. Since farming the land was the only productive activity that occupied the farmer, **agricultural man ate to live and lived to eat, making life start and end with food.**

However, after agriculture was established and its culture and economy were developed, the pace of social change slowed, causing life conditions to become steady and seem perpetual. Most forces of change were at the time either dormant or yet to be born or resistant to change like religion. Nevertheless, the later centuries of the agricultural age witnessed important developments that included the transformation of religion into an institution with authority, the development of writing and reading, the formation of states, the invention of the wheel, the expansion of trade, and the incorporation of money and merchant life into the life of society, which caused the pace of change to accelerate. Around the middle of the fifteenth century, the agricultural society entered a transitional period leading to the industrial age.

In the second half of the eighteenth century, the production of manufactured goods emerged in England as the most important economic activity. This development heralded the coming of a new era, the industrial age with its own civilization, and the dawn of rapid change in all aspects of life. The coming together of major social, cultural, polit ical institutions, new ideas, technological inventions, scientific discoveries, geographical discoveries, and the sociocultural transformation caused by the religious wars is what is called the Industrial Revolution. It was a revolution that changed the mode of production and production relations, forcing all aspects of life to change drastically, profoundly, and irreversibly. The Industrial Revolution emerged as a continuous process of change that seemed to have no end in sight. "Our fathers started the revolution, and we are still living it. We could not stop it even if we wanted to."[5] In fact, the Industrial Revolution ushered in a wave of comprehensive change that transformed all aspects of life in every industrial state.

For example, workers were no longer free to determine their working hours and how to perform their work; tasks were assigned, working hours were imposed, and hierarchical relationships within the workplace were enforced. Income was tied to work, making survival a function of work availability and worker's capacity to work long hours and endure the pain of performing repetitious, often boring tasks. For the first time in history, the new worker could own neither the place of work, the means of production, nor the end products he produced. His only source of income was his labor and time, and labor and time were the only commodities he could trade. Industrial man, as a result, was transformed through manufacturing into a machine, causing work to become the focal point of life. **Industrial man works to live and lives to work, causing life to start and end with work, even for the majority of the rich capitalists**.

As the Industrial Revolution advanced, it expanded and diversified economic and financial activities, causing new jobs to be created and more people to be involved in manufacturing. This in turn created a need for people to perform related tasks such as plant supervisors, accountants, transportation and trade managers, banking and investment officers, technicians, innovators, and engineers to develop new products. Consequently, a new class of largely urban dwellers was born; it was neither rich nor poor but in between. Because of its unique social position and functions, the new class shared neither interests nor traditions with the rich or the poor; it had to develop its own way of life and claim its place in society as a middle class.

The evolution of the industrial age strengthened the economic forces and institutions of society, giving capital and the capitalist system prominent roles in the industrial society's life and its people. The capacity of the forces of the economic process to contribute to every human activity has enabled the economic process to grow stronger and become more visible and eventually replace the political process as the most dominant process in society. As a consequence, the representatives of this process were able to claim special rights and privileges not available to the rest of the population.

In the 1990s, industrial society in general and American society in particular began to experience a new wave of fundamental change or revolution. This revolution was driven by knowledge, particularly the information and communications revolutions and the Internet, which caused the economy to shift fast from the production of manufactured goods to the production of tradable services. In the middle of the 1990s, the Knowledge age began to impose its logic on the prevailing ways of living and states of living, causing all aspects of life to undergo fundamental and irreversible change. In the United States, "service employment accounted for 80% of employment in 2000. More people were at the time working in doctors' offices than in auto plants and more in laundries and dry cleaners than in steel mills."[6] In 2017, the employment in the service sector was growing, while employment in agriculture was down to 1.66% of the labor force. Due to this development, the knowledge man is being transformed into a thinking machine, ***he learns to live and lives to learn***, causing his life to start and end with learning. Consequently, whoever fails to continue learning will lose his source of livelihood, and with it, his social existence.

At the time of writing this book in 2022, I feel that the transitional period leading to the knowledge age is still incomplete; it needs about 3 more years to reach its end. However, many far-reaching changes have already occurred and can be seen at all levels of individual and societal life. Values, traditions, and convictions that provided the social glue that kept families and communities tied together throughout the agricultural and industrial ages have begun to fracture. Basic assumptions that helped historians, economists, sociologists, political, and strategic thinkers to define and analyze social, political, and economic units such as the nation state, national economy, culture, and class have been partially or totally invalidated.

The first transitional period from the tribal to the agricultural age lasted about 3000 years. The second transitional period separating the agricultural from the industrial age lasted about 300 years, from the middle of the fifteenth century to the middle of the eighteenth century. The current transitional period separating the industrial from the knowledge age is expected to last about 30 years. This suggests that the length of each successive transitional period is about 10% of the preceding one. If this observation could be used as a rule of thumb, the knowledge age should become a reality around 2025. This simply means that we are entering a never-experienced age of continuous change and transformation that no one can manage or predict what it will bring tomorrow.

In concluding this chapter, it is important to reiterate that each stage of development represents a unique civilization with its particular society, economy, and culture. Since each civilization comes after a difficult transitional period, every transitional period, viewed from a wide angle, represents a *historical discontinuity* that causes the history of the passing era to come to an end. As one history ends, its logic becomes irrelevant, and the wisdom of the past becomes of little or no value to people of the new age. Transitional periods are battlegrounds where war is waged between old and new values and ideas, between forces of stability and continuity, and others of innovation and change. Such periods are workshops for destructive creativity, where creativity is a tool of destruction and destruction is a condition for further creativity. As the third decade of the twenty-first century begins, almost all nations of the world seem to be, as Matthew Arnold once remarked, "wandering between two worlds, one dead, the other unable to be born."[7]

In the tribal age, the tribe represented the unit of society and the entire society, in fact until the eighteenth century; no tribe recognized a state or respected political borders. In the agricultural age, the tribe could not survive because the need for it disappeared, causing the clan or the extended family to take its place. Due to the appearance of the state, the clan became the unit of the agricultural society. In the industrial age, the clan had to disappear because there was no place for it or need for its services; it was replaced by the nucleus family. As the knowledge age advances, it becomes clear that the individual is fast becoming the unit of the new age, replacing the family of the industrial age which replaced the clan of the agricultural age which replaced the tribe of the tribal age.

Notes

1. Mohamed Rabie, *Global Economic and Cultural Transformation*, Palgrave Macmillan, 2013, 21–42.
2. Ibid, p 11.
3. Jared Diamond, *Gun, Germs and Steel: The Fate of Human Societies*, W.W. Norton, 1999, 92.
4. Jack Weatherford, Savages and Civilization, 49.
5. Charles Van Doren, *A History of Knowledge*, 1991, 263.
6. Joel Rogers and Ruy Teixeira, "America's Forgotten Majority," *The Atlantic*, June 2000, 69.
7. Lenichi Ohmae, The End of the Nation State, 1994, 10.

CHAPTER 4

Societal Processes of Change

Abstract This chapter tries to explain the process of transformation throughout history and identify the tools that facilitated the transformation process; it invents four tools; the sociocultural, the sociopolitical, the socioeconomic, and the infomedia processes. It also explains how these processes were developed, how and why the forces of each process were forced to cooperate with the forces of the previous process, how and why each process overwhelmed the forces of the previous processes, creating the conditions and interrelations that manage the affairs of all societies today.

Keywords Cultural · Political · Economic · Media · Nationalism · Colonialism · Marxism · Liberalism · Conservatism · Ideological · Globalization · Capitalism · Consumerism · Environmentalism

The societal processes of change and transformation are tools I invented to identify the forces that led change and transformation throughout history and influenced its direction; that is the forces that charted the path of the historical process. In the not-distant past, gifted leaders, natural resources, strategic locations, empires, creative minds, grand ideas, and religions played important, at times decisive roles as agents of change and societal transformation. Lately, however, the roles of all such agents have

M. Rabie, *A Future Economy for All*,
https://doi.org/10.1007/978-3-031-42957-6_4

diminished, and the roles of certain societal processes have been enhanced at their expense. Nevertheless, from the birth of early human societies, these societal processes have played major roles in causing sociocultural, sociopolitical, and socioeconomic change, both positive and negative.

The societal processes of change and transformation are four processes, the sociocultural process, the political process, the economic process, and the infomedia process; this process includes both the traditional mass media and the social media. These processes evolved as self-regulating mechanisms to facilitate the introduction of change and manage its consequences. Unlike social systems that man builds and controls to manage the life affairs of society, the societal processes do not abide by certain rules or laws and are not subject to control by any authority.

Since these processes evolved one after the other, the role that the dominant societal process plays in the life of society reflects the philosophical orientation of society and the developmental stage of its economy, culture, political system, and life conditions in general. Together, these four processes form the larger framework within which all institutions and social systems function, and through which all change is introduced and managed in society.

The sociocultural process was the first process to emerge in history, followed centuries later by the political process. These two processes, working together, have concentrated on continuity and stability rather than on change and transformation; as a consequence, they were able to dominate societal life for countless generations without causing noticeable change. The economic process emerged slowly and grew gradually during the second half of the agricultural age, but gained momentum after the Industrial Revolution, causing fundamental changes in the life of industrial society. However, as the economic process approached maturity in the middle of the twentieth century, the infomedia process emerged to challenge its dominance and lead societal change by influencing public opinion, people's attitudes, lifestyles, and ways of thinking. Nevertheless, their competition did not last long due to the nature of their functions; today, the economic and infomedia processes work together and reinforce one another, concentrating on change and transformation rather than on continuity and stability.

The sociocultural process produced great ideas and ideologies, of which religion is the most prominent one. The political process produced great political and military leaders, empires, and political philosophies, of which nationalism, colonialism, racism, and democracy are the notable ones. The economic process produced great technologies, entrepreneurs, countless inventors, as well as mercantilism, capitalism, Marxism, and communism. Meanwhile, the infomedia process has produced and continues to produce great technological innovations, global cultures, virtual communities, and cultural ghettos, while systematically destroying many cultural and ideological barriers on the one hand, and facilitating economic integration across continents, and causing cultural globalization on the other. In addition, the consequences of the actions of these two processes have caused the concepts of national identity and national interest to be undermined.

Each societal process has specific tasks to perform, objectives to pursue, and logic to follow. But since no change can occur without affecting the relative roles of most players in society, every process affects the other processes and is affected by them. Nevertheless, in each civilization one process distinguishes itself as the major vehicle facilitating change and influencing its direction. While the sociocultural process dominated the life of the tribal and early agricultural societies, the political process dominated the lives of mature agricultural and early industrial societies; and the economic process dominated the life of mature industrial societies. Today, the infomedia process, in association with the economic process, determines the nature and direction of change in almost all societies, particularly societies passing through the transitional period from the agricultural to the industrial age and from the industrial to the knowledge age. In fact, transitional periods are laboratories for change and transformation beyond the ability of any state or international organization to control.

Each societal process sought the approval and support of the process that preceded it; but as the new process gained enough power, it sought to dominate the other and succeeded in achieving its objectives. For example, as the political process emerged, it sought the approval and support of the sociocultural process; the union of these two processes led initially to strengthening the sociocultural forces; but slowly and gradually the sociocultural forces were undermined, causing the authority and rationale of politics to be strengthened. When the economic process emerged, its union with the political process led initially to the strengthening of the political forces, but slowly and gradually the power and rationale of politics was undermined, causing the power and rationale of economics to be strengthened. Today, the infomedia process is cooperating more and competing less with the economic process; so if the current merger trend continues and the commercializing of media organizations intensifies as expected, the economic and infomedia processes are likely to form a powerful societal process beyond serious challenge by any other societal process.

In each age or stage of civilizational development, the process that enjoys most authority in society claims most of the talent available and employs it to serve its interests. In the agricultural age, the sociocultural process attracted the most talented people at the community level to serve religion and spread the faith. When the political process became dominant, it attracted the most talented individuals available in the regions under state control, employing them as bureaucrats, military commanders, tax collectors, and political thinkers. As a result, the sociocultural and political processes denied society the opportunity to use its talent to develop the economy, technology, and education, directing talent instead to ensuring cultural continuity and maintaining political stability. Today, the economic process attracts most talented people at the international level, employing them in industrial production, inventions, scientific research, and technological development. Meanwhile, the infomedia process, along with the economic one, attracts almost all the talent in industrial and knowledge societies, as well as a good portion of the talent available in the developing world, employing them as researchers and innovators in the fields of finance, information technology, telecommunications, and technical and marketing services. As a result of these transformations, little creative minds are left to provide humanity with strategic thinkers and visionaries.

Social Change

Throughout history, it was the societal processes of change and transformation that caused the upheavals that humanity witnessed and gave us the world we live in today. The sociocultural process worked relentlessly to transform the hunter-gatherer bands into stable communities, using kinship, traditions, and belief systems to give each community an identity of its own; and that caused values and cultures to form the basis of association in older times. The forces of the political process, motivated by ambitions and lust for power were able to reshape the world, create nations, states, and empires that facilitated cultural interaction and helped expand trade. The forces of the economic process, motivated by lust for money, developed many products and created new institutions that impelled people to build new associations on the basis of interests, causing all nations to eventually become economically interdependent. The forces of the infomedia process work today to link individuals together and create virtual communities on the basis of either shared hobbies and interests or shared convictions and transform the world into a global village that progressively renders political borders less meaningful, national cultures less particular, and ideology less sacred.

All socioeconomic activities everywhere involve the forces of the four processes of change and transformation. When relationships between these processes are well defined and in balance, which rarely happens, stability prevails in society for a short time. But when one process attempts to expand its role at the expense of one or more of the other processes, instability ensues. Such instability, however, is neither permanent nor necessarily bad; it often represents a transitional period where both conflict and change are occurring simultaneously and influencing one another. But for some balance to be restored, a new relationship has to be established around new bases that change the relative roles of the forces involved.

Today, global developments and local conditions are pressuring the economic process to be more sensitive to local needs, while calling for more attention by the political process to national issues. Unemployment, poverty, crime, and environmental neglect accentuate the need for both the political and economic processes to cooperate and give more attention to local issues. In the meantime, economic and military competition, and the spread of conflict and violence around the world, and the international migration of people due to severe economic and political conditions call for all processes to get more involved in facing the many challenges that threaten human life as we got accustomed to.

In the thick of confusion and chaos caused by the transition from the industrial to the knowledge age, the forces of the sociocultural process are forced to abandon their traditional role of unifying communities and nations around shared values and traditions. Instead, they are compelled to move in two contradictory directions at once; this move is dictated by the need to accommodate the desires of a globalized economic process on the one hand, and to respond to the need of minorities for cultural recognition and political freedom on the other. While the development of a global culture based on the values and lifestyles of Western capitalism, consumerism, and liberalism accommodates an economic process eager to expand internationally, the revival of minority subcultures serves to strengthen minority participation in the political process, in the hope of influencing change in their favor. The triumph of US President Donald Trump in the 2016 elections reflects, at least partially, the success of a reinvigorated conservative cultural minority in influencing the political process.

The infomedia process, meanwhile, serves as the main vehicle facilitating the movement of the other processes in their relentless pursuit to influence societal change in their favor. While the forces of the infomedia process often expose the failure of the political process to attend properly to local and international issues, it helps open new markets and identifies new global opportunities for the economic process to explore. It also enables the forces of the sociocultural process to develop a global culture and invigorate numerous subcultures at all levels. As it assumes the traditional role of the political party in debating public issues, the infomedia process tends to expose the shortcomings of the economic process, especially its lack of commitment to national environmental causes. In addition, the infomedia process undermines the power of the sociocultural process, denying it the opportunity to maintain national unity and preserve people's identity.

Interaction among the four societal processes, as explained above, causes the balance of relationships in society to live a life of continuous change and transformation. During periods of profound change, such as the transition from one civilization to another, relationships tend to become rather chaotic, causing older rules and regulations to become less effective. Older theories of thought and models of analysis and roadmaps become outdated before new ones are developed to deal with the changed situations, causing confusion and oftentimes a loss of direction as well. At such times, intellectual activity and creativity are usually revived and pushed to go beyond the known and the traditional; and this usually causes the conventional wisdom and its logic to be undermined, and new ways of thinking and worldviews to appear and be legitimized. In transitional periods, however, it is always easier to explain emerging situations than to control them or predict their outcomes.

Chaos and order always exist together in one world. They are two sides of one social process, and neither one can survive long without the other. Order without chaos, just like cooperation without some competition, characterizes social systems that lack dynamism and cannot develop or adapt to new circumstances. On the other hand, uncontrolled chaos, just like cutthroat competition, characterizes social systems that are badly conceived and mostly unproductive, and thus headed toward disintegration. As Lester Thurow once said, "America has more than enough chaos to be creative, but too little order to use its ideas in the most efficient ways. Japan has more than enough order to be efficient, but too little chaos to be creative."[1]

A new theory of social change to explain chaos and order and how and why they erupt is badly needed to bridge the widening gap between the reality of politics and the imperatives of economics in the age of knowledge that promises to live a continuous life of change and transformation. Such a theory should make it possible for us to use the certainty of order to regulate chaos, use the dynamics of chaos to transform order, and employ the propensities of both chaos and order to resolve conflict and make economic and technological progress a reality shared by all. The "train of time theory" outlined in my book, "*Global Economic and Cultural Transformation*" is an attempt to explain social transformation throughout history by placing chaos and order, conflict, and change, in their proper historical and societal contexts. This theory should enable all concerned parties to make an educated judgment regarding both the past and the future and how they relate to one another.[2]

Notes

1. Lester Thurow, Building Wealth, *The Atlantic Monthly*, June 1999, 63i–4.
2. Mohamed Rabie, *Global Economic and Cultural Transformation*, Palgrave Macmillan, 2013, Chapter 7, 107–127.

CHAPTER 5

Culture and Civilization

Abstract This chapter tries to explain the difference between "Culture" and "Civilization," because without understanding the meaning of each concept and how they relate to each other, the evolvement of history and the fates of civilizations and cultures and societies would not be understood correctly.

Keywords Webster dictionary · Civilization · Culture · Society · Community · Traditions · Customs · Belief systems · Literature · Media · Science · Technology

This is a short essay to explain the concepts of culture and civilization; the reason for this explanation is due to the fact that most people and even social scientists do not differentiate between the two concepts and without understanding the meaning of each concept and how they relate to each other, the evolution of history and the fates of civilizations, cultures, and societies would not be understood correctly. Many ordinary people and even social scientists often use the words culture and civilization interchangeably, as if they have the same meaning.

Although the two words have similar definitions that tend to confuse many people, the connotations of the two words represent distinct concepts. Explaining the meaning of each word and the importance of

M. Rabie, *A Future Economy for All*,
https://doi.org/10.1007/978-3-031-42957-6_5

its connotation requires an explanation of how they relate to each other in a historical context. Such a clarification is important to understanding the course of human development over time and to identifying the issues causing cultures and their followers to often misunderstand each other, and at times to clash with one another.

Webster's Encyclopedic Dictionary defines "civilization" as an advanced state of human society, in which a high level of culture, science, industry, and government has been reached."[1] An alternate definition by the same source refers to civilization as "modern comforts and conveniences, as made possible by science and technology." As for "culture," it is defined as "the sum total of ways of living built up by a group of human beings and transmitted from one generation to another."[2] Generally speaking, "culture stands for the way of life that a group of people follows and defines the social cement that binds its members together, forming a community or society."[3]

The first definition of civilization as the achievement of "a high level of culture, science, industry and government" considers culture, just like science and industry, one component of civilization, rather than its equal or its other face. This definition suggests that culture does not include science, industry, or government; it includes only such intangible things that may be transmitted from one generation to another as traditions, customs, literature, beliefs, and value systems. Culture, defined by Constantine Zurayk, is "the sum of the creative achievements of the human spirit in society."[4] In Thomas Sowell's formulation, culture "involves attitudes as well as skills, languages, and customs."[5] Michael Naumann, Germany's former Minister for Cultural and Media Affairs, said "culture is a symbol for spiritual innovation, for satirical laughter, for imagination, for intellectual challenge – but also for comfort, for relaxation and for all those forms of entertainment that do not automatically dull people's minds."[6]

Since civilization includes culture and culture is only one of several components of civilization, neither concept should be used to refer to the other. Using both concepts interchangeably therefore confuses issues related to both culture and civilization and makes it hard to understand how each concept relates to the other, and this makes it difficult to identify the place of culture as well as the place of civilization in the past and present history.

Culture, as defined above, concerns itself with the quality rather than the quantity of what society has developed over time in the visual arts, literature, values, traditions, and similar fields of human endeavor. It refers to "the sum total of ways of living built up by a group of human beings," interacting with each other in what is called society. This suggests that culture includes traditions, customs, attitudes, laws, belief systems, worldviews, social activities, ways of thinking, and relationships developed by a group of people or by a nation over time and transmitted from one generation to another. Culture, therefore, is particular, rather than universal. It is a product of people living and working together for a very long time in what we call society.

Civilization, which refers to both the quality and quantity of human achievements, is a product of people interacting with each other and with nature over long periods of time and in countless places. It therefore tends to underline the comforts of life that are attainable through industry, science, technology, as well as culture. These are developments that in and of themselves reflect the accumulation of knowledge developed by all peoples throughout history. Because the interaction of humanity with nature is meant to discover nature's secrets and laws and exploit its resources, economic factors, and technology become decisive forces in making and shaping civilizations. Civilization, therefore, is produced by humanity and belongs to all peoples of the world; culture is produced by society and therefore belongs to one nation. Consequently, culture is more particular and portable, while civilization is more global and non-transferable; the first is communal; the second is universal.

It is clear from the above explanation that civilization includes the material and non-material achievements of all peoples, while culture is confined to the non-material accomplishments of one people only. Since culture is a component of civilization and one of its many aspects, a civilization can and does produce more than one culture. Being an attribute of one civilization, culture owes its very existence and basic traits to the particular civilization that produced it, and not to any other civilization.

Because cultures are products and attributes of civilizations, their developments follow that of their mother civilizations. This is not to say that cultures do not influence or impact the development of their mother civilizations. On the contrary, after a civilization is fully developed, its cultural component usually assumes an active role in shaping the direction and influencing the pace of change in society. Cultures, being the total of ways of living, shape the way younger generations think, influencing their attitudes toward other cultures, the environment, science and technology, industry, the workplace, education, and other peoples. The most important elements of culture, I believe, are the values it espouses and the attitudes it impels people to adopt, particularly toward the environment, work and time, science and technology, and the pursuit of happiness and material gain.

Being a product of people's interactions with one another, the development of culture as an important aspect of life had to wait for societies to be formed. Only after agriculture was developed and human settlements appeared did culture begin to develop in a systematic way and influence change in society. Since the age of agriculture lasted about ten thousand years before the Industrial Revolution began, all cultures produced during that period were products of one single civilization, the agricultural one, and therefore were similar to one another. "Until comparatively recently in human history, all humans had the same subsistence pattern. In a certain sense, they all shared a similar, though not identical culture."[7] Describing life conditions and the way of life in Pacoma, a village in Bolivia, Jack Weatherford wrote, "In many ways Pacoma seems typical of village life across South America as well as throughout India, China and Sub-Saharan Africa."[8]

Each of the so-called civilizations of the ancient past is acknowledged as such because of its noted achievements in cultural attributes, economics, science, technology, and political and military organization. All great civilizations, regardless of their time, duration, or comparative level of achievements, have produced refined cultures in the form of works of art, literature, architecture, and behavior and belief systems. No group of people was able to join the ranks of the acknowledged civilized nations at any time without enjoying a noteworthy cultural life.

Cultures, therefore, are products of civilizations; and their levels of achievements are functions of the achievements of the civilizations that produce them. Advanced civilizations produce refined cultures, and refined cultures reflect the achievements of advanced civilizations. The material and non-material achievements of civilizations thus go hand in hand, and their internal dynamics and mutual influence are what make progress, stagnation, and/or regression possible.

One last word on civilization and culture and how they relate to each other. The only civilization in history whose people had the ethical and moral values to be humanely civilized was the agricultural civilization because these values needed a family environment to develop and cherish. Subsequent civilizations were more scientifically, technologically and economically advanced but lacked the ethical and moral values to be civilized. Economic progress leads people to become greedy and materialistic, and technologically advanced weapons lead people to become colonizers determined to subjugate poor people, steal their natural resources, and deny them their human rights, even the freedom to manage their life affairs. Therefore, Western civilization, being materialistic and expansionist, could not develop the ethical and moral values to be civilized.

Notes

1. *Webster's Encyclopedic Unabridged Dictionary of the English Language*, New York: Portland House, 1989, 270–271.
2. Ibid, 353.
3. Stuart Chase, *The Proper Study of Mankind*, New York: Harper & Row, 1962, 61.
4. Constantine K. Zurayk, "Cultural Change and Transformation of Arab Society," in *The Arab Future: Critical Issues,* ed. Michael C. Hudson, Washington, DC: Georgetown University, 1979, 17.
5. Thomas Sowell, *Race and Culture*, New York: Basic Books, 1994, 10.
6. Michael Naumann, "A Dialogue of Cultures," *Deutschland,* No. 3, June/July 2000.
7. Jack Weatherford, *Savages and Civilization,* New York: Ballantine Books, 1994, 26.
8. Ibid, p 45.

CHAPTER 6

Materialism in Historical Perspective

Abstract This chapter focuses on explaining the role of materialism in society; materialism seams to have lately acquired the role claimed by religion in a traditional agricultural society. People are rich and poor, not because God and religion had ordained it as old societies believed, but because economics and knowledge and culture and greed have determined it. Man, consequently, is seen as the master of his fate, and that neither God nor religion has anything to do with his lot in life.

Keywords Materialism · God · Religion · Community · Ghettos · Poverty · Property · Middle class · Values · Socialism · Capitalism · Democracy · Justice · South Korea · Saudi Arabia

Materialism has lately acquired the role claimed by religion in agricultural society; it has become the major driving force in life. People are rich and poor, not because God and religion had ordained it as old societies believed, but because economics, knowledge and culture have determined it. Man, consequently, is seen as the master of his own fate, and neither God nor religion has anything to do with his lot in life. In the meantime, individualism has become the philosophy of the knowledge age, causing poverty and community and even nation to become minor issues of no particular concern to the elites controlling the economic and infomedia

M. Rabie, *A Future Economy for All*,
https://doi.org/10.1007/978-3-031-42957-6_6

processes. As a result, national cultures are being divided into subcultures, national societies are gradually disintegrating into sub-societies and cultural ghettos, and the "national interest" is fast becoming a vague concept that is hard to define and harder to understand and relate to.

Every human being comes to life with a strong desire to own things, which leads him to invest a lot of time and energy to acquire whatever assets are available, desirable, and reachable. In tribal times, man had very little things to acquire, because he was always on the move and could not carry most things he would have liked to own. But when man began to build and live in permanent agricultural settlements, the institution of private property appeared and caused wealth to become a major source of power shaping social relations and social structures. Meanwhile, the hamlets and villages which man settled in enabled him to own and enjoy some material things.

However, private property remained simple throughout the agricultural age; it did not exceed a piece of land, primitive tools, some money, and a little family house. About 250 years ago, man moved from the agricultural to the industrial age, leading him to become more materialistic and possessive. Consequently, private property expanded to include industrial plants, tangible assets, technological gadgets, and things usually used to enhance life comfort and expand and diversify the range of recreational activities open to people. As the knowledge age advances, man's desire to own more wealth has increased, and materialism has become the ultimate source of individual satisfaction and social status. This has enabled the wealthy to become more powerful and socially respected than the religious and political men of decades ago.

The absence of the institution of private property in tribal times made society classless, and that helped its members to avoid exploitation and slavery. But after the building of agricultural settlements and farming the land, private property was transformed into a socioeconomic force that divided society into two classes, a rich class of landlords, and a poor class of small peasants and slaves. Consequently, exploitation appeared, allowing the rich to enslave the poor and acquire more wealth and power at their expense. The industrial age expanded the range of economic activities, which facilitated the creation of a relatively large middle class. Due to its social status and economic weight, the middle class was able to play a constructive societal role, facilitating mobility socially, politically, and economically.

But with the discrediting of socialism, the move of China toward capitalism, and the arrival of the knowledge age, change in the major Western states began to accelerate. Most states moved to relax financial and trade regulations, giving the rich and large corporations the freedom to pursue their economic and social goals, dismantle labor unions and exploit every opportunity and everyone in sight. As a result, the middle class began to lose its power and social and political influence. To justify their deeds, the rich began to blame the poor for their poverty and bad living conditions, as if discrimination and lack of adequate education and equal opportunity do not matter.

The concentration of power in the hands of a small political, economic, and media elite has enabled the rich to confiscate most of the rights of the poor and powerless, in violation of the principles of democratic and human rights. In the meantime, greed, jealousy, and envy intensified in every society, leading the rich to ignore the ethics of fairness and justice, while forcing the poor to ignore honesty and, at times, dignity to satisfy their desires. Consequently, the rich driven by greed and lust for money and power; and the poor driven by need and jealousy, and lust to acquire social status by owning some of the gadgets that the rich own have caused evil inclinations to become major forces motivating most people to work, invest, compete, cheat, deceive and sometimes steal to get ahead.

Today, all societies are experiencing a dramatic decline in the influence of values, business ethics, and the community spirit that governed the lives of preindustrial societies for generations. Although many forces could be blamed for causing this unhealthy development, the overall movement toward individualism and materialism on the one hand, and the abandonment of spiritualism and collectivism on the other are the major forces that stand behind the retreat of traditional values and ethics. "While rich individuals try hard to acquire more material things, most poor people try harder to imitate the rich but do little to acquire more knowledge and reclaim their rights. As a consequence, more emphasis is being placed on consumption and the appearance of wealth than on production and education and the essence of living meaningful and productive lives."[1]

Joseph Schumpeter argued more than 60 years ago that the most damaging consequences of capitalism are the negative effects it has on the values that support the social order in society.[2] "But what Schumpeter had failed to notice is that cultures have a great capacity to adapt, and that values are able to transform themselves and accommodate economic and technological change associated with capitalism. The values that prevailed in the 1950s did not disintegrate, and the social order they supported did not collapse suddenly; rather, new values emerged slowly, and a new social order formed gradually, creating new socioeconomic and sociopolitical relationships compatible with a manure industrial economy. However, the new values came to justify the new reality and thus to side with the rich and powerful. But the excesses of materialism induced by the advancement of industrial capitalism forced society to intervene and enact new laws that made the system less exploitative and more respectful of the common good."[3] Meanwhile, capitalists' need to interact with workers and bargain with them in good faith, was instrumental in facilitating the emergence of a rather equitable social order which most Western societies enjoyed for three to four decades, ending with the transition from the industrial age to the knowledge age in the mid-1990s.

Ideas, ideological convictions, traditions, and values on the one hand, and science, technologies, institutions, and interests on the other have had a competitive relationship throughout history. Wherever beliefs, values, traditions, and ideological convictions dominate, freedom is restricted, and technologies, institutions, and economies are used primarily as tools to foster ideology and enhance the power of its leadership. Iran, North Korea and Saudi Arabia are examples of states where technology and economy are used to tighten the ruling elites' grip on power and hinder sociocultural and socioeconomic transformation. In contrast, wherever institutions, technologies, interests, and science dominate, freedom prevails but social justice often suffers. Therefore, reducing the influence of traditional values and ideological convictions has become a prerequisite for meaningful societal transformation and moving toward freedom. On the other hand, meaningful socioeconomic change to reduce the influence of the rich and powerful has become a prerequisite for creating just societies.

When social life is largely static, ideological convictions can and often do change living conditions; but when social life is largely dynamic, conditions can and often do change ideological convictions. In the knowledge age, where change is unstoppable, changing living conditions are destined to shape and reshape convictions without interruption. Therefore, human values and belief systems are destined to change and end the reign of ideology and the terror of ideological leaders. However, the road to upending the terror of ideology is expected to be long and hazardous; Islamic radicalism and anti-globalization in the East, and anti-emigrant and racial discrimination in the West suggest that restoring social peace at the national level and balance of economic power at the global level is difficult; causing the world's poor to suffer most. The election of President Trump who imposed tariffs on China, and Britain's exit from the European Union show that globalization is retreating, and the old world order is disintegrating, and this means that the nation state needs to adjust its policies to reflect this reality. All states should move vigorously to change the global social order to be just and sustainable.

Until a few decades ago, able and charismatic leaders have symbolized the convictions that left a lasting impact on the lives of most people. However, no leader could claim greatness and lead unchallenged without being associated with an ideology or unusual but convincing convictions. This is why the recent decline in the role of ideology has been associated with a decline in the influence of political leaders. The future therefore is unlikely to witness the appearance of a great leader or a grand ideology able to change the course of history in a meaningful way. Historical records seem to suggest that no nation had been able to enjoy freedom of expression and institute democratic traditions and respect for human rights under the rule of charismatic leaders claiming greatness or divine authority. Charisma in society has always been in conflict with freedom and institutional bureaucracy because the latter works to enforce the law, not to promote leaders. In societies still living in preindustrial times, institutional bureaucracy is very weak, allowing political leaders to be absolutists. Absolute rulers, remarked Ottaviano Fregoso five centuries ago, are "always finding themselves obeyed and almost adored with such reverence and praise… They are subject to such boundless self-esteem that they take no advice from others,"[4] and therefore they have no respect for the rights of anyone of their subjects.

Knowledge in the past had been more spiritual and human than materialistic, more liberal than conservative, and more pluralistic than exclusive and ideological. Due to these unique characteristics, knowledge was able to play a constructive role in helping the poor and the needy, solving social and economic problems, and inspiring change and progress. In contrast, the bulk of knowledge in the new age has become more materialistic than anything else; it is composed primarily of technological gadgets and information and computer programs and applications. While such products and information have high economic returns, they have little spiritual and humanistic returns; they tend to encourage individualism and reinforce greed and consumerism. In addition, they make information subject to manipulation by the media and other social actors to suit every strain of thought and business concern. As a consequence, the new knowledge and the people who produce it and the elite who control it have become less committed to humanistic causes. Therefore, to address the daunting challenges facing humanity, intellectuals and thinkers need to be conscious of the changing nature of knowledge and the socioeconomic developments that engulf our lives.[5]

This makes it clear that every society in history has been more materialistic than the preceding one, and more inclined to exploit other people for the sake of wealth and power. In fact, at every turn in our social history, wealthy individuals, groups, and nations have resorted to power to suppress others and discriminate against them, employing economic and military power and violence to exploit the powerless and impoverish the poor. So, every step toward more materialism power, and individualism is a step away from the values of equality, social justice, fairness, freedom, and respect for human rights and the dignity of man.

Since economic development relies heavily on scientific discoveries and technological innovations and capital accumulation, education and creativity have become major sources of wealth. People, to work hard and acquire more wealth and get the satisfaction they aspire for, need to feel that they can keep most of the money they earn. If the wealth of a nation were to be divided equally among all citizens, no one would probably work for anyone else, causing the economy to stagnate. So, without the material incentive individual drive to excel would be hampered, and societal development would be retarded. Nevertheless, private property and wealth and the power they generate should be regulated and directed toward enriching the collective life of people, not used by the powerful as tools to exploit the poor and weak and deny them their social, cultural, economic, political, and human rights.

Notes

1. Mohamed Rabie, *A Theory of Sustainable Sociocultural and Economic Development*, Palgrave Macmillan, 2016, 77.
2. Schumpeter, Capitalism, Socialism and Democracy, 1950.
3. Mohamed Rabie, *Saving Capitalism and Democracy*, Palgrave Macmillan, 2013, 57.

4. Mohamed Rabie, *Global Economic and Cultural Transformation*, Palgrave Macmillan, 2013, 77.
5. Ibid, p. 186.

CHAPTER 7

The Dialectical Relationship between Power, Wealth, and Knowledge

Abstract This chapter tries to proves that there is a dialectical relationship tying Power, Wealth and Knowledge to each other. This relationship started in the tribal age and continues today. However, while power was the means to obtain wealth in the tribal and agricultural times, wealth was the major tool to acquire power and power was the major tool to acquire knowledge in agricultural times. Today, knowledge has become the major source of wealth, and wealth has become the major source of power. This means that while power in older times lead to knowledge through wealth, knowledge today leads to power through wealth also. So history shows that power leads to wealth, and wealth leads to knowledge, and knowledge translates itself into wealth, and wealth translates itself into political power and social status.

Keywords Religion · God · Faith · Miracles · Injustice · Poverty · Slaves · Values · Ghettoes · Intellectual · Cultural · Rich · Poor · Ignorance · Knowledge

During the era of tribalism, which witnessed the emergence of signs of civilization in its primitive form, wealth and knowledge were virtually absent from the life of tribal man, which enabled the traditional social forces to control the sources of influence and power in society. Old age

M. Rabie, *A Future Economy for All*,
https://doi.org/10.1007/978-3-031-42957-6_7

and the wisdom of the past were the major sources of both power and knowledge in tribal societies. In the absence of wealth and income, which are the bases of social classes, tribal society escaped the division of its members into social classes; as a consequence, members of each tribe enjoyed equal rights, causing exploitation and slavery to play a minor role in the life of tribal societies in general.

In the agricultural era, private ownership of agricultural land and water sources emerged as an institution with legitimacy, giving the powerful groups that became farmers to seize the most fertile land and monopolize its use. Consequently, the agricultural society was divided into two social classes, one is rich, and the other is poor. While the rich class consisted of landowners who owned large farms and estates and slaves, the poor class consisted of small farmers and agricultural workers and slaves. As the powerful took possession of slaves to work on their farms, they were able to devote part of their time to think about life and the universe, and to engage in intellectual and cultural activities that enabled them to create and possess some knowledge. With the emergence and entrenchment of social classes, however, the rich were able to exploit the poor, and the powerful were able to enslave the weak. Consequently, poverty, injustice, and need prevailed in agricultural societies for many centuries.

On the other hand, the emergence of religion in agricultural society about five thousand years ago as a sacred social and cultural institution enabled religion and its men to become an important force, playing a pivotal role in the life of agricultural society. Religion urged the rich to sympathize with the poor and asked the strong to help the weak. In addition, religion claimed to know the truth about life and the afterlife, which enabled it and its men to influence agricultural cultures, especially the society's traditions and values. This process came through the addition of new beliefs and rituals and rites that accepted the agricultural way of life and recognized farming of the land as a legitimate activity; and that made it easy for all members of agricultural society to accept religious teachings and rituals and follow its men.

But since religious knowledge cannot be proven, all stories about gods and prophets and angels and miracles became claims that may be true and may be false. But in the absence of scientific knowledge to contradict religious knowledge, agricultural man was easily convinced to believe and be content; he was enticed by the magic of religious stories and the peace of mind that religions provided and that enabled the religious institution to acquire a high moral position in society and employ it to acquire wealth and influence to shape the social and cultural life of agricultural societies for thousands of years to come.

During the age of industry, which witnessed the development of scientific knowledge and technology and the establishment of good schools and universities, wealth began to shift from the domain of farms and land to the domain of manufacturing plants and financial institutions. In the meantime, knowledge and technology became important tools to improving labor productivity and raising the efficiency of the manufacturing process and causing economies to grow and diversify. In the light of the availability of good schools and universities, wealth became a means to acquiring scientific knowledge by attending the new schools and universities and traveling around the globe. So, acquiring scientific knowledge became accessible through regular study, practical applications of theories and technologies, and relying on creative minds. As a consequence religious knowledge was exposed as mere claims that have nothing to do with science or work or production. In the meantime, people with knowledge were able to get good jobs and acquire wealth and prestige and play increasing roles in shaping society and its culture and economy.

Due to this development, the status of religious claims and clerics declined considerably, causing both religious knowledge and religious men to lose a great deal of the social status and privileges they enjoyed during the agricultural age. Consequently, a large portion of the industrial society lost faith in religion and became more interested in life than in the afterlife, which led them to become more materialistic and less spiritual. With the passing of time interest in acquiring more wealth became an obsession that undermined the values and ethics of industrial communities in general.

On the other hand, the age of industry witnessed the division of society into three distinct social classes: a rich bourgeois class, a poor working class, and a middle class that was neither wealthy nor poor. This class emerged as a result of the expansion and diversification of the economy, especially in the manufacturing and services fields; services included financial, commercial, healthcare, education, administrative, and other services. Although this division led to stabilizing the industrial society, it created a rather difficult balance between the various social classes, because their interests were contradictory and could not be reconciled. Nevertheless, all classes were keen to protect democracy because it gave them the opportunity and the means to pursue their goals and protect their interests. So balance came through each party's determination to pursue its interests by recognizing the two other parties and respecting their rights to pursue their own interests.

In addition, the industrial society witnessed the institutionalization of the democratic idea and its transformation with the passing of time into a system of government that provided freedom for most people, and a measure of social justice, which came through the elimination of slavery, undermining the power of the strong to exploit the weak, and the creation of new and sometimes rewarding jobs. Although these arrangements caused injustice to decline in general, the democratic system failed to establish equality of rights as a fact of life. Nevertheless, the greatest accomplishment of democracy was to transform itself into a sociocultural value or an attitude that caused almost every member of the democratic society to view everyone else as equal who deserves equal social, political, and economic rights.

In the age of knowledge, which is evolving at an astonishing speed, wealth moved from the domain of factories to the domain of knowledge in all its forms. The main components of knowledge in this age are financial and consulting services, information, social media, communications, artificial intelligence, and creative ideas that include many computer applications. In light of the success of knowledge in assuming the most important position in society, it has become a source of wealth and an effective means of acquiring power. Because of the pervasive characteristics of knowledge, the new society is no longer a class society in the traditional sense. It has become a society composed of sociocultural groups that have varying levels of education, different cultures and subcultures, multiple interests and hobbies, and diversified national and global affiliations, with a focus on abstract material interests. This has caused a precipitous decline in the importance of traditions and religion in the life of the knowledge society in general, and the distancing of knowledge from its human message in particular.

In the meantime, the division of the knowledge society into sociocultural groups based mainly on culture, rather than wealth and income, has caused the role of nationality and loyalty to country and people to be vastly diminished. Whereas wealth in previous eras was fixed as farms and land or manufacturing plants, scientific knowledge, financial services, information technologies and computer applications are fast changing their faces and moving from one company to another and from one country to another. But as wealth and income gaps widened in the knowledge society, the previous social differences were compounded by educational and cultural differences. As a result, cultural ghettos multiplied and spread widely, poverty and ignorance became intrinsic features of every society, the middle class lost much of its status and influence, and belonging to a particular community and nation disappeared. Consequently, the role of democracy as a fair system of governance declined, causing the foundations of justice and equality to be undermined. This has led to depriving many people of their full political, social, and economic rights.

So, to restore balance and fairness to the knowledge society, the cultural ghettos need to be eliminated by destroying the walls that separate the many groups from one another and create a new social glue to tie them together. However since the walls that separate cultural ghettos from each other are made of knowledge and cultural barriers, they have become hard to overcome and harder to eliminate. This means that the only way to restore balance and social peace is to develop a new social order that guarantees fairness and justice for all peoples of the world. This makes the taming of the rich and powerful a must, and facing this difficult challenge an ethical duty.

Returning to the distant past, we discover that power was the means to obtain wealth, and this happened in both the tribal and agricultural times. While invasion and looting were the means to obtain wealth in the tribal era, confiscating fertile land and water resources and owning slaves were the means to obtain wealth in the agricultural era. However, the ability of the agricultural society to produce a surplus of food caused the idea of progress to be born. The wealthy who owned slaves to work on their farms and serve in their homes were able to find the time to think about life and the universe and thus produce some knowledge. This means that power led to acquiring wealth, and wealth leads to producing knowledge. In the knowledge age in which we live today, knowledge has become the major source of acquiring wealth, and wealth has become the major source of acquiring power. This means that the dynamic relationship between power, wealth, and knowledge turned society's movement upside down; instead of starting with power to reach knowledge through wealth, progress has made the process start with knowledge and reach power through wealth.

So history shows that power leads to wealth, and wealth leads to knowledge, and knowledge translates itself into wealth, and wealth translates itself into political power and social status. As a consequence, people and states that are wealthy are able to acquire power and use it to influence national, regional, and international change in their favor; states and people who lack wealth and power cannot influence global or regional change to serve their interests. This means that people who lack wealth and knowledge are helpless, unable to free themselves from being mere tools to serve the interests of the wealthy and powerful groups and states. These facts must be seen by the powerful, rich groups and states as reasons justifying domestic and international radicalism and violence.

For poor states seeking to develop their economies and societies, they need to adopt new ideas and strategies that start by acquiring knowledge and building the educational and research institutions of society, because such institutions are the means to acquire, produce and disseminate knowledge in society. The age of starting the development process by developing the agricultural sector, raising the productivity of farmers, and building factories and centers to train workers is gone. India gives a good example of a nation that focused on acquiring more knowledge, particularly in the field of information technologies and achieved great success. However since knowledge covers all scientific fields and influences all aspects of life, India's scientific progress made the development of the agricultural and industrial sectors easier than before. This means that emphasis on knowledge does not neglect the agricultural or the industrial sector; it makes development a comprehensive societal process that raises the level of interest in both sectors while treating the present and the future as integral parts of a strategic project under construction.

CHAPTER 8

Decline of Democracy and Capitalism

Abstract This chapter tries to expose the problems that are facing the democratic and capitalist systems and explain why both systems have lost their capacity to manage the political and economic affairs of the societies they control, particularly the American society. Though both systems were capable of doing what was expected of them between the 1950s and the early 1980s, they began to lose that capability with the adoption of market capitalism and allowing money to control the political system and corrupt most politicians. Therefore, both systems need restructuring or replacement. Public doubt about their ability to manage American affairs is reflected in the continuous infighting between the Democrats and the Republicans as well as in public opinion polls and participation in elections.

Keywords Capitalism · Democracy · Ideology · Intellectualism · Racism · Discrimination · Violence · Equality · Responsibility · Governance · Hierarchical · Horizontal · Mercantilism · Nationalism

A careful look at the world situation will reveal that we live in a world characterized by chaos, loss of direction, extremism, the revival of racism and discrimination, as well as war and conflict. While the rich societies of the West pass through a state of confusion and loss of direction, the

M. Rabie, *A Future Economy for All*,
https://doi.org/10.1007/978-3-031-42957-6_8

poor states of the East pass through a state of widespread ignorance, corruption, and civil conflict. Ideological intolerance, a tendency toward isolation from the rest of the world and a focus on money has caused our world to lose its old sense of community and spirituality, giving individualism, materialism, greed, and racial discrimination the upper hand in shaping national and group cultures, directing economic activity, and influencing political governance.

This causes most people to feel that they are strangers lost in a strange land without a compass to guide them, and that leads them to search for leaders to take them back to the safety of the past. But such leaders, realizing the desperate need of the masses for help, are moving to confiscate the freedom and will of the people seeking help, and turning them into herds of sheep following a cruel shepherd carrying a big stick in his hand and a deformed mind in his head. In the meantime, traditional intellectuals, feeling frustrated and unable to comprehend the new life complexities, have abandoned their social responsibilities toward the masses. But to regain a sense of safety and comfort, they join one ideological group or another, not knowing that the age of ideology is gone. In most instances, the absence of justice and awareness leads such intellectuals to fall into the arms of religion and its men to shelter themselves from having to face challenges they do not understand, and deal with an uncertain future. Promoting the ideas of certain religious men and thinkers who lived and died a long time ago becomes their new claim to knowing the truth and enjoying peace of mind. But by so doing, they commit themselves to living in the dark tunnels of history and the graves of dead ideas.

This feeling of loss and bewilderment is enforced by a lack of people with the knowledge and foresight to explain the emerging new situation and lead the masses to realize what to expect and not to expect in the near future, and how to deal with the unexpected. In the meantime, some of the traditional intellectuals and racists have taken advantage of this situation to promote discrimination against the other and blame the other for whatever the masses fear and complain about. This has caused many people on all sides of the racists' lines to lose their sense of humanity and humility. As a consequence, a new class of racist leaders has emerged to monopolize political power, control cultural activities, economic resources, the mass media and employ all these means to gain as much wealth and power as possible at the expense of everyone else.

In most Third World states, the political elite moved in the 1970s to build the official organs of repression and control: a well-equipped police force, a national army, a bureaucracy, an intelligence apparatus, and official media, and employ these organs to humiliate the people, falsify their consciousness, and convince them to accept their lot in life and be content. To remain in control, the ruling elite used the state intelligence organs to spy on intellectuals and advocates of freedom and limit their capacity to spread awareness in society and help people to understand the complexity of life and deal with it rationally. As a result, poverty, fear, ignorance, corruption, and oppression spread, causing most societies to remain mired in backwardness, and miss all the developments that the world has witnessed since the Industrial Revolution.

Since I believe that justice and freedom are fundamental human rights and that without justice and freedom, no life is worth living, the proposed political and economic systems in this book focus on the values of justice and freedom. The establishment of social systems based on equality of opportunity and equal rights and responsibilities has become a prerequisite for invoking the sociocultural and socioeconomic transformations needed to achieve both human and material progress. Although the proposed systems embody the spirit of democracy as a sociocultural value, and the spirit of capitalism as an economic production and management system, the proposed systems differ from the current democratic and market capitalism systems in their composition and institutions and the role each plays in the life of society.

Fair systems of governance must ensure the participation of the masses in the political process, and the liberation of people from ignorance, need, discrimination, and fear; justice prevents the rich and powerful from exploiting the poor and the weak while guaranteeing equality of opportunity. Free and just societies that ensure equality of social, political, and economic opportunity pave the way for continued sociocultural, socioeconomic, and sociopolitical transformation. This causes society to become a dynamic beehive that does not stop working and giving. Human experience suggests that people of the West came close to achieving justice and freedom only after the separation of church and state around the middle of the seventeenth century, and the development of the democratic system of governance in the late eighteenth century.

On the other hand, it is necessary to recognize that the democratic and capitalist systems were born almost at the same time, which made them twins that can hardly be separated. Though both systems were instrumental in helping most Western societies to make great scientific and economic and technological progress for two centuries, they began in the 1980s to ignore the principles of justice, freedom, and equal opportunity. But as Western societies began their transition from the industrial age to the knowledge age in the mid-1990s, democracy and capitalism began to lose the essence of their social mission. The twin revolutions of information and communications on the one hand, and the great advancement in the fields of science and technology on the other, gave capitalism and democracy the opportunity to ignore business ethics and feel free to exploit the poor, violate the rights of the weak, and undermine the public interest. This means that changing the current situation and restoring a measure of justice and freedom requires the restructuring of the democratic and capitalist systems. In fact, as explained earlier, each civilization produces its own society economy, and culture, causing the pillars of the passing civilization to lose their validity and ability to do what is needed and expected of them. Therefore the choice we face today is to transform the capitalist and democratic systems to produce stable and safe societies, tolerable cultures, and growing economies, or allow the chaos and loss of direction that characterizes transitional periods to shape our societies, cultures, and economies.

During tribal times, the tribal society had no state with laws to govern its affairs; therefore tribal customs and norms were developed as social tools to manage tribal affairs and solve conflict within the tribe peacefully. In the agricultural community, and before the state and the law came into existence, values, traditions, and religious ethics emerged slowly to regulate individual and group behavior and manage community affairs. In the absence of the state and the law, the tribal Sheikh became the head of the tribe, and the clan chief became the head of the agricultural community, making the social structure in both societies hierarchical. In the industrial society, both the tribe and the clan lost their social roles and therefore had to disappear; they were replaced by the nucleus family. In the light of the existence of the state and its organs and institutions and the law, the social structure of the industrial society became horizontal; and with the emergence and continued growth of civil society organizations, the hierarchical structure disappeared, and because the tribal customs and agricultural traditions had also to disappear, social, religious, and political freedom spread, and democracy deepened its roots in industrial society.

Since all civil society organizations are based on professional ties shared hobbies, and common interests, the social structure of all such organizations became horizontal. With this development, the democratic system was slowly transformed from being a system of governance only to being a sociocultural value that accepts and respects equality of rights and obligations, giving birth to the citizenship concept. While democracy spread, capitalism slowly emerged as a system of economic production and management, causing the industrial society to be divided into three socioeconomic classes. In the meantime, the adoption of mercantilism as an economic philosophy, and nationalism as a sociopolitical philosophy gave birth and legitimacy to the colonial enterprise. The colonial enterprise was designed to search for natural resources and new markets to exploit. Due to the nature of mercantilism and nationalism all classes and institutions of the industrial society, including the church and its men, participated in the colonial enterprise, which is considered the most oppressive and unjust form of rule in human history.

In the meantime, the continued existence and functioning of the tribe and the clan in tribal and agricultural societies hindered the transformation of the social structures of both societies from being hierarchical to being horizontal; and that prevented the emergence of social, religious, and political freedoms, as well as the freedom of speech and association. As a consequence, neither democracy as a system of governance nor as a sociocultural value could develop in those societies. This caused the tribal and agricultural societies to lag behind the industrial societies and suffer the indignation of poverty and ignorance and colonialism. Even the tribal and agricultural societies that have a lot of money due to the discovery of oil in their countries could not develop culturally, economically, or scientifically; they remained mired in backwardness after decades of financial wealth and becoming aware of the Western experience. In fact, the abundance of money caused what I call the "petroleum society" to develop a culture of consumption at the expense of the culture of production.

We need to understand that any analysis and critique of democracy and capitalism, and any speculation about the future of either system will have to focus on the American experience; otherwise, no evaluation will be sufficient to guide us into the future we must build. The American democratic and capitalist experience derives its importance from being the oldest democracy in modern times, and the capitalist system that built the largest and most advanced economy in the world, and the most powerful army in the history of mankind.

While most Western societies were enjoying rising standards of living and expanding economies, the socialist system instigated by Marxist ideas after the Bolshevik Revolution of 1917 in Russia came to pose a serious challenge to capitalism and its promoters who feared socialism. In fact, socialism compelled the Western democratic states in general to adopt progressive social and economic policies that included raising taxes on the rich, designing and implementing new programs to protect the public, expanding public education, empowering workers, and creating welfare programs to help the poor, the needy, the unemployed and the elderly. Western states also began to promote the concept of 'equality of opportunity' to counter the Marxist concept of total equality. Both the upper and the middle classes in the West provided, rather willingly, the money needed to finance the welfare programs because they hated socialism and its premise of class conflict and promise of a classless society.

Decades later, however, neither the middle nor the rich class was willing to finance the mushrooming welfare programs. While the financial price of those programs was increasing without an end in sight, Marxism and its socialist system were failing and no longer feared by the rich and the upper middle class. In order to accomplish their objectives of lowering taxes and reducing spending on social programs, the upper and, to a lesser extent the middle classes began to call for smaller governments, less state intervention in public life, less economic and financial regulations and less taxes; some also called for more restrictions on immigration. Money and the media were used to manipulate public opinion, distort facts, and pressure both the executive and legislative branches of government to accommodate the demands of the rich and others who were aspiring to become rich. These were changes that paved the way for a new culture based on individualism, where individuals and corporations have rights but little social responsibilities.

In the wake of the dramatic ending of the Cold War in 1989, democracy and capitalism emerged as the most promising political and economic systems, if not the only legitimate ones. They appealed to the majority of people everywhere, and particularly to those who lived the longest and suffered the most under the authoritarian rule of communist regimes and Third World dictators. As communism was collapsing under the weight of its own failure, the Western media was busy promoting both democracy and capitalism, causing the birth of a large international wave promoting democracy and respect for human rights. In the meantime, the World Bank the International Monetary Fund, and the US government were busy pressuring most states to adopt the free market philosophy; however, no country that listened to this advice was able to develop its economy or free its people from the debt burden. In fact, global debt continued to grow, reaching about $100 trillion in 2019. As a consequence, the global economy failed to resume normal growth rates, and all heavily indebted rich and poor nations failed to free their people from the growing debt burden.

Money, without which neither the state nor politics can function properly, was used in America to manipulate and at times bribe politicians, making elections an unequal contest between those who have money and others who have little or no money. Senator Richard Durbin admitted in 2010 that the barons of the banking sector "frankly own the US Congress."[1] According to the Washington Post, the cost of the 2016 presidential elections reached $6.5 billion, though President Donald Trump did not spend much. According to CNN, the cost of the 2018 congressional elections exceeded $5.7 billion. "Spending in the 2018 elections for Congress topped $5.7 billion, making the battle for control of the House and Senate the most expensive midterm ever."[2] However, the cost of the 2020 elections exceeded $14 billion. "Political spending in the 2020 election totaled $14.4 billion, more than doubling the total cost of the record-breaking 2016 presidential election cycle".[3]

And with the advent of globalization and free trade in the 1990s, economics was able to triumph over politics, causing a significant setback for both democracy and capitalism, as well as for the middle class and the nation state. Consequently, the political process lost its independence and freedom, which forced it to abandon its traditional societal role. Meanwhile, money and the rich were allowed to determine what was fair and what was not, what was good for society and what was not, and what was in the national interest and what was not. In fact, the national interest, due to the involvement of money in elections, and the adoption of free trade and free markets, was transformed into a vague concept hard to understand and harder to relate to.

So, the triumph of economics over politics in the 1980s and beyond made the political process a tool in the service of the leaders of the economic process. As a consequence, democracy was hijacked, causing its ability to do the things it is supposed to do to be undermined. Eric Alterman says, "When attempting to determine why the people's will is so frequently frustrated in our [democratic] system, one must turn first and foremost to the power of money; the system is rigged, and it's rigged against us."[4] Decades ago, Walter Lippmann said, "In the cold light of experience, he [the private citizen] knows that his sovereignty is a fiction. He reigns in theory, but in fact, he does not reign. Contemplating himself and his actual accomplishments in public affairs, contrasting the influence he exerts with the influence he is supposed to exert according to democratic theory, he must say of his sovereignty what Bismarck said of Napoleon III, at distance it is something, but close to it, it is nothing at all."[5]

While politics was losing its independence and objectivity due to the influence of money, the state was losing its ability to manage the economy, care for its citizens, and define the national interest. At the same time, the public, particularly the middle class, was losing its sovereignty and influence; it could not resist the temptations of the new luxuries of life and avoid debt and manipulation by the agents of the economic and infomedia processes. On the other hand, capitalists, supported by a conservative political movement during President Reagan's administration, began in the 1980s to dismantle labor unions and state regulations, causing the middle class to lose much of its social status and political power. "It was unions that made the American economy work for the middle class, and it was their later decline that turned the economy upside-down and made it into a playground for the business and financial classes,"[6] said Kevin Drum. As a result of these developments, democracy was weakened, and its major institutions ceased to function properly.

In the knowledge age, the socioeconomic gaps that separate the rich from everyone else are growing wider; while the sociocultural divides that separate the many cultural and ethnic groups from one another are growing deeper. In the meantime, the state is getting weaker and less able to control its economy and play its traditional role in ensuring equal opportunity. Meanwhile, a rich and powerful class determined to influence politics and corrupt politicians has prevented the major centers of social and political power from intervening to facilitate the building of a new social order compatible with the economic and social imperatives of the new age. As a result, the need for a new social order capable of balancing the relationships between the rich and powerful on the one hand and the poor and powerless on the other has remained unfulfilled. While budgets for social and educational programs are being cut, taxes on the rich are being reduced, and the poor are being isolated and neglected. Failure to rebalance class and group relations and interests will ultimately lead to social unrest and possibly violence. France, England, Italy, Greece, and other states give us a picture of what might happen in America in the future.

While the rich under the old capitalist system had concentrated on expanding manufacturing that drove economic growth and created millions of jobs for the unemployed and, in the process, enhanced the national wealth, the super-rich of the knowledge age are focusing on creating financial products and computer applications and artificial intelligence that contribute to building personal wealth, often at the expense of the national wealth. Because the first capitalist class had to interact with millions of workers on a daily basis, it became aware of the need to ensure the welfare of its employees and the development of the communities hosting their operations. The new class of the super-rich, in contrast, does not interact with workers or even with most of its customers, because it derives most of its wealth from dealing in virtual products within virtual communities away from the public eye.

Due to their shared interests and interconnectedness, the super-rich have developed a unique global culture having its own values, traditions, ethics, language, and even vocabulary that others have difficulty understanding, and because the majority of its members have a house everywhere and no home anywhere, they have become aliens having no loyalty to any particular place or nation or ideology or cause; the only god they know, and worship day and night is money. To remain faithful to that god, they are willing to manipulate, cheat, steal, exploit, and conspire against others to get closer to him; so in case he gets sick or dies they will be in a position to take his place and play his role. Having gained a lot of wealth and power, the super-rich are employing money to influence politics and corrupt politicians to ensure the continuation of the current unjust and unsustainable social order.

Notes

1. Michael Kazin: "Building a Movement by Offering Solutions," *The Nation*, September 6, 2010, 17.
2. https://www.cnn.com/2019/02/07/politics/midterm-election-costs-topped-5-7-billion/index.html
3. Karl Evers-Hillstrom, Most expensive ever: 2020 election cost $14.4 billion, February 11, 2021. https://www.opensecrets.org/news/2021/02/2020-cycle-cost-14p4-billion-doubling-16/

4. Eric Alterman: "Kabuki Democracy," in *The Nation,* September 2, 2010, 12.
5. Richard Harwood, "The Messenger Shouldn't Bear all the Blame," *The Washington Post,* Feb. 15, 1996, A 21.
6. Kevin Drum: "Plutocracy Now," *Mother Jones*, March/April 2011, 24.

CHAPTER 9

The Folk Political System

Abstract This chapter explains the need to construct a new political system that gives every citizen a role in shaping it and benefiting from it. The folk political system could be defined, using the same words used by US President Abraham Lincoln in 1863, as a "system of the people, by the people, for the people." However, the structure of the folk political system is different from the existing one in ways that make it less vulnerable to corruption and the influence of money and the misuse of political and economic power. The need to change this system and most other systems is due to the fact that no system can keep its validity while all facets of life continue to change and be transformed.

Keywords Folk · Democratic · Constitution · Lobbyists · Validity · Plurality · Militarized intellectuals · Press · Conservatives · Corruption · Civilization · Minorities · Tolerance · National interest

The folk political system could be defined, using the same words used by US President Abraham Lincoln in 1863, as a "system of the people, by the people, for the people." However, the structure of the folk system is different in ways that make it less vulnerable to corruption and the influence of money and the misuse of political and economic power. In addition, the changing living conditions of the last three decades have

M. Rabie, *A Future Economy for All*,
https://doi.org/10.1007/978-3-031-42957-6_9

made certain components of the traditional democratic system in need of restructuring or replacement, because no system can keep its validity while life conditions continue to change; even religions were forced to change to adapt to changing times and living conditions. Besides, while making the folk system less vulnerable to corruption, it invents new ways to guarantee wider representation of all sectors of society and prevents the misuse of power; in fact, the system introduces the idea of sharing power among all components of society. The system is structured in a way that allows the state to be a republic or a constitutional monarchy. This is important to making the folk system applicable and acceptable to societies where vertical social structures still exist.

Since life circumstances change causing relationships in society to change, democratic systems also change to stay relevant and fulfill their obligations. Therefore, democracy must be seen as an evolving sociopolitical process that affects and is affected by the values and attitudes of people and their worldviews, as well as by the economic and cultural conditions on the ground. Since cultures are products of civilizations that continue to change, the institutions of democracy are shaped by the historical experiences and the socioeconomic and sociocultural circumstances that govern how civilizations develop, and because different societies have had different historical experiences and live under different conditions, democracy expresses itself in varied forms and political arrangements. The analysis that follows focuses on the American experience for three reasons.

a. Democracy as a political system was first established in America over two centuries ago.
b. The American society never lost faith in the democratic system, and despite the system's apparent shortcomings, it functioned fairly well for almost two hundred years without significant change; and
c. The United States has been the undisputed political, economic, scientific, and military leader of the democratic world for almost a century.

Nevertheless, the American democratic experience shows that members of the political, economic, and media elites were able to gain extra powers and use them to claim special rights unavailable to the general public. Elites are even able to use their power to deny some people opportunities to which they are entitled in a democratic, open society, and use the media to inflame the passions of people, brainwash many of them, and achieve certain goals that contradict the public interest. This suggests that the economic, political, and media elites have replaced the ruling families of older times in repressing and manipulating people's needs and fears and denying them some of their legitimate rights.

So, before outlining the structure of the envisioned folk political system, it is necessary to explain the reasons behind the declining validity of the traditional democratic system and how it lost its essence of social responsibility and national mission. Though American democracy started with the adoption of the constitution in 1787, it took almost 200 years for the system to recognize the right of all people to participate in the political process and be protected by the law. However, the system lost its essence and social mission while it was being implemented.

Western political thinkers suggest that a truly democratic system must have three major requirements to function properly:

1. Political plurality that guarantees minority participation in the political process and gives all citizens a real choice between competing political parties with different social and economic programs.
2. The presence of a middle class large enough, confident enough, independent enough, and conscious enough to know its interests and protect them; and
3. A free press that facilitates freedom of speech and informs the public, and plays an active, yet neutral role during elections and political campaigns.

However, my experience of 50 years of studying, living, teaching, and traveling in the United States and several European countries has given me the opportunity to see democracy in action and participate in the American elections. On the other hand, a unique life experience, lasting many years of living, studying, teaching, and traveling in several Middle Eastern, North African, and Asian countries has enabled me to look at other competing systems from the outside, not just from the inside. As a consequence, I believe that democracy cannot function properly without a fourth condition: the presence of a culture of tolerance.

Political Plurality

As the religiously and nationally conservative American forces began to promote an anti-liberal, anti-science, and anti-intellectual agenda in the late 1970s, they used the economy, the federal budget, immigration, national security, and Islam as a cover to advance their agenda. The organizing principle of this group is discrimination against everyone who disagrees with its worldview, causing political thinking to become largely totalitarian and discriminatory. By the end of the twentieth century, the political process in America was controlled by small groups of politicians, media personalities, rich and greedy businessmen, professional lobbyists and image-makers, retired army generals and intelligence officers, political consultants, and militarized intellectuals. Though members of these groups often disagree and fight with one another, they show no real interest in reforming the system or relinquishing power.

Consequently, political plurality in America ended as the twenty-first century was being born, causing political parties to be reduced to little more than a convenient framework to facilitate elite competition and cooperation, and justify exclusion of all other citizens. American political parties are no longer popular movements representing competing sociopolitical or socioeconomic views capable of giving the public a real choice. Instead, they have become two ideological blocks working to mold and remold people's culture, confiscate political and economic power, and employ it to foster their interests and the interests of their financial backers. There is no doubt that the American Democratic Party talks about the declining fortunes of the middle class but has done almost nothing to enable this class to recover some of the power and social status it had lost.

In fact, having only two parties contending for political power in society is not adequate to provide political plurality; there is a need for at least one more major party to give people a reasonable choice. A third party will not only expand the range of choices, but it will also reduce the chances of one party winning the majority of votes to rule unchallenged. Since elected members of both parties tend to respond to the interests of the rich and ignore the interests of the poor and the middle class, neither party represents the American people or works to protect their rights or advance the national interest. In addition, no political party could have the backing of the majority of people no matter how many votes it may get in an election cycle, or how many members it has in congress. Since

50–60% of the American people normally vote during presidential elections and a smaller percentage participate in congressional elections, no party can get a majority. Any majority that a party may get is a majority of voters participating in an election cycle, who often represent a minority of the American people.

The Middle Class

One of the serious problems facing all democracies today is the gradual deterioration of the status and influence of the middle class. What makes this problem more serious is the fact that governing is increasingly being monopolized by a small, rich, self-centered, and largely isolated class, and because this class uses money and the media to manipulate people and falsify their consciousness, democracy continues to fail people and gradually lose their trust and support. Since money took over politics in the 1980s, the middle class has suffered major setbacks that weakened its ability to play its traditional role in life. Industrial workers were pressured to abandon unions, industrial jobs were shipped overseas, and incomes have failed to keep pace with rising costs of living. Consequently, the American scene has witnessed a sharp decline in the efficiency and legitimacy of representative government. According to a survey of US public opinion published in February 2019, confidence in US institutions reached new lows. Confidence in the government was 35% and no confidence 63%; confidence in the executive branch (president) was 42% and no confidence 58%; confidence in Congress was 40% and no confidence 59%; and in the mass media, confidence was 45% and no confidence 54%.[1]

The middle-class in the democratic West in general and in America in particular has become like a runner who runs on a fast moving treadmill. He runs faster and faster just to stay in place and avoid falling off the treadmill track. But struggling to stay in place, while others keep marching along accumulating more wealth and gaining more power, causes the middle class to become exhausted, weakened, and dizzy. The unfortunate members of the middle class who are vulnerable because of their old age, poor health, inadequate income or knowledge, or minority status are falling off the treadmill track and joining the ranks of the poor and powerless.

As for poverty in America, reports indicate that 13.8% of men, and 16.3% of women lived in poverty in 2016. The poverty rate among children was 21.2% (15.3 million kids), or one child in every five. In addition, in 2014 the National Center on Family Homelessness found that nationwide, 2.5 million children experience homelessness every year. As for poverty among the races, according to the 2016 US Census Data, the highest poverty rate was found among Native Americans (27.6%), with Blacks coming second (26.2%), and Hispanics having the third highest poverty rate (23.4%). Whites had a poverty rate of 12.4%, while Asians had a poverty rate of 12.3%.[2] However, the rates changed in 2021, causing the national poverty rate to be 12.8%, but significantly different for the nation's oldest and youngest populations. The child poverty rate for people under age 18 was 16.6%, 4.2% higher than the national rate, while poverty for those whose ages are 65 years and older was 10.3%. But though the national child poverty rate was 16.9%, there was considerable variation among states within America, ranging from 8.1 to 27.7%.[3]

Free Press

By the time the Cold War ended, the mass media had become too powerful and too commercialized to pay serious attention to national or international issues, except to issues that serve the interests of its corporate owners and sponsors. Two decades later, the media stopped showing interest in informing or educating the public or even giving people the opportunity to express their opinions. As the media was gaining more power to collect, analyze, manipulate, and disseminate information regarding most aspects of life, its power was increasingly being concentrated in the hands of a few conglomerates and a small group of media elite. The failure of the media to predict the results of the 2016 elections that brought President Donald Trump to power indicates that it has lost touch with the people. In fact, not a single public or private institution, including the hundreds of centers of strategic studies and the official intelligence agencies was able to predict the outcome of the 2016 election. This proves that all components of the ruling elite have lost touch with the people they claim to represent and serve.

Since the adoption of the free market economic philosophy in the 1980s, the Western media in general and the American media in particular moved to consolidate their operations by forming media empires dedicated to making money. However, the most damaging impact of the merger of capitalism with the media is seen in the relentless campaign of the new alliance to subordinate human behavior and ethical values to the economic imperatives of money making. People's fears, instincts, emotions, desires, and even evil tendencies are being awakened to create new exploitable needs. Excitement is heightened and envy is provoked to make more money for the rich and powerful. As business concerns, the mass media has become more responsive to the demands of the stock market and its corporate investors and sponsors than to issues of concern to the public, such as poverty, the middle class, education, healthcare, the deindustrialization of America, and the consequences of war and peace. To meet the expectations of the stock market, media entrepreneurs felt a need to favor profitable programs that feature violence, drugs, and sex, even programs that are socially harmful and morally corrupt. In the meantime, social media is collecting information about adults and children alike and selling it to merchandisers; making the private lives and secrets of young men and women and even children commodities to sell to the highest bidder, and in the process harm the future of many of them.

Today, while the economic process and its barons are given the freedom to pollute local, national, and global environments, and money is given the freedom to manipulate elections and corrupt politics and elected officials, the media is given the freedom to falsify people's consciousness and pollute the minds of whoever takes its views and news seriously. People who enjoy success and have wealth are right; people who experience the pain of failure and suffer poverty are wrong. "In post-democratic America, we understand that the rich are rich, and therefore good; the poor are poor, and therefore bad,"[4] said Liesl Schillinger. No one asks or even seems to feel an obligation to ask how the rich could make so much money or how ethical were the means used to make it. Consequently, a new subculture emerged where greed is considered good and wealth is the primary criterion to differentiate between success and failure, smartness and dumbness.

Elections and the Media

US public opinion polls indicate that conservative Americans are increasingly focusing on narrow issues; they listen to radio talk shows and media personalities that propagate their points of view only. Generally speaking, conservatives everywhere watch news and TV programs that are biased in favor of what they believe in, and not what they need to know. Instead of seeking new knowledge and ideas, conservatives often seek what validates their beliefs and convictions. Leaders of the Democratic and Republican parties have formed cultural ghettos where they live intellectually and think and plan their actions in isolation away from the public eye. In 2020, not a single democratic candidate out of the 20 presidential hopefuls asked potential voters for ideas; everyone asks for donations only. People as far as the ruling elite are concerned are a herd that must be led and not consulted. This attitude means that no candidate has learned the lesson of the 2016 election; ignoring people is what gave Trump the opportunity to appeal to the neglected and win the presidency. Back in 1992, I wrote in my book, *the New World Order*, that most White Americans look at everyone who does not look like them and say, "you may belong to us, but you do not belong with us."

Former US President Gerald Ford described American election campaigns as "candidates without ideas, hiring consultants without convictions to run campaigns without content."[5] That was in the middle of the 1970s. By the end of the twentieth century, the situation had gotten much worse, causing all hopes of reforming the political system and reviving democracy to vanish in the thick clouds of greed and corruption. While democracy is supposed to be a process of renewal and change, it has become a process to recycle failed and failing politicians and ideas. Both George W. Bush and Barack Obama did a great job recycling America's failed politician, hiring people who served many years earlier under previous administrations to deal with problems and challenges they had never dealt with or even imagined happening. And with every administration the situation got worse, causing hope of reforming the system to die in silence.

Due to a biased media, freedom of speech in America has become practically non-existent; it is limited to those who own a media establishment and others who manage it for them. People who do not own a major newspaper, a magazine, or a radio or television station have little or no freedom of speech. Freedom of speech is not only the freedom to say what you think privately, but to say it publicly via a medium that enables you to express your ideas and views openly and reach your targeted audiences, which only the media can facilitate but rarely allows to happen. The Internet and social media are the only means that have the potential to provide alternative venues for the free expression of opinions. However, their independence is being undermined by the commercial objectives they seek to accomplish, while the integrity of the people in charge of them is being compromised by business interests and ideological attachments. This is why the Facebook management resorts sometimes to closing the pages of people with political views that do not agree with, and why Google's computers are programmed to change the contents of political statements that Google's managers do not like.

Today, the infomedia is able through a selective process to inform and misinform to deceive people and lead them to follow what it advocates. While faked news is a fact, the more dangerous and harmful act is hiding the news the public needs to know to make rational decisions; so by hiding certain facts from the public, the media undermine the election processes and the human interest. Committed intellectuals espousing unconventional ideas are denied access to the media and thus freedom of speech, leaving the general public with no choice but to follow what the media is saying. Even academics who express views that deviate from what the barons of the media and their business sponsors promote are often excluded and denied freedom of speech, and because media organizations have different and often contradictory views regarding most social and economic issues, the public and its views have fractured, causing confidence in government to decline. This has left money and demagogues in charge of swaying voters one way or the other. According to ThoughtCo, a person interested to become US president needs about $1 billion to run a campaign that has a good chance of winning the elections. As for members of the Senate and Congress, the average spending has reached almost $20 million for a senate seat and almost $1.7 million for a congressional seat. This means that an incumbent senator needs to raise over $9130 a day of his six years in office to collect enough money to run a successful campaign; and for a member of Congress, he has to raise over $2,300 a day of his two years in office.

Tolerance

"There is no democracy without democrats, that is, without a specifically Democratic Man that desires and shapes democracy even as he is shaped by it,"[6] wrote Francis Fukuyama. But in order to nurture the development of democrats who desire and promote democracy, certain conditions must exist; people must be able to appreciate the value and promise of democracy, which they cannot appreciate without having the right education, the right information, the right attitudes, and a culture of tolerance. Yet, "no society can be called tolerant or intolerant without reservations; each society tolerates certain things, resists others, and discriminates between many more. For example, Western societies in general are more tolerant of political dissent and uncommon social behavior than eastern societies, but less tolerant of racial diversity. Arab and Muslim societies, in contrast, are generally more tolerant of racial diversity, but have almost no tolerance for political and ideological dissent."[7]

However, no society or culture has arrived at its current state of tolerance without passing through difficult times and experiencing painful changes. Religious tolerance in the West, for example, was not possible before the Protestant Reformation and the religious wars that swept Europe in the seventeenth century; and democracy was unimaginable before the Industrial Revolution and its mode of production and the social and economic structures it produced. Lack of democracy as a political system, and lack of support for it as a sociocultural value in most Third World states must therefore be linked to the absence of both religious reform and industrial social formations. A society where ideology dominates culturally and rules politically, and where economic activities are largely agricultural and limited in scope, can neither nurture true tolerance nor produce a workable democratic system.

For people to be tolerant and democratic they have to accept the right of others to be different; they have also to act on the basis of understanding that their beliefs and values are an expression of their choices, not of a universal truth that others must accept. In addition, people must understand that their attitudes and views are expressions of a reality that changes as economic conditions and interests and social relations change, rather than being convictions and eternal facts that do not change. Since ideologies, by their very nature, tend to claim that they, and no one else, know the truth, they represent a formidable obstacle to sociocultural transformation, and therefore to tolerance and democracy. Ideologies almost always cause people to become narrow-minded, more rigid and less free and tolerant, and more inclined to discriminate against the other and accept non-democratic rule.

Sociocultural groups, unlike socioeconomic classes, tend to share more traditions and values and convictions than interests, and because of that, they include the rich, the poor, and many more in between. The Republican Party in American is a sociocultural group whose organizing principles are small government, low taxes, and free markets. Other minorities in the West, such as North Africans in France, Indians in Britain, Turks in Germany, Koreans and Chinese in America, are sociocultural groups that include the rich and poor of their own peoples. However, within each group, the rich and poor rarely interact with one another; at times, the rich use whatever wealth and power they may have to exploit the poor and powerless members of their own communities. Nevertheless, both the rich and poor of those minorities share very little with the rich or the poor of other minorities living in the same countries where they live. Democracy which gave people the freedom to voice their ideas and differences on the one hand, and instant communication channels to link together and develop particular views and identities on the other, have combined to make this unique development possible. Today, every society in the world is experiencing its segmentation into socioeconomic classes and sociocultural groups that have little in common to form homogenous communities.

Since the traditional middle class in the West is slowly but methodically being dismantled rather than strengthened, and because the political party has lost its traditional role in society to the media, the two pillars of Western democracy are crumbling and cannot be saved without drastic change. Moreover, current trends of sociocultural, socioeconomic and sociopolitical change indicates that the transition from the industrial to the knowledge age is creating new situations that serve the interests of the media, economic monopolies, and the rich and powerful only; and that these situations are least conducive to the revival or even sustenance of either the middle class or political plurality. What we have today and should expect to have more in the future is sociocultural diversity, not sociopolitical plurality, a weaker not stronger middle class, a more biased not fairer media, and more bigotry and discrimination and less tolerance.

Structuring the Folk Political System

The practical application of people's participation in the political process can be carried out according to several formulas, with each having its own requirements and consequences. However, in the light of the increasing complexity of life and the continuous interaction of people with their rulers, it is necessary to devise a new formula that allows people to participate in the political process, ensure the separation of religion from state, and open the way for the people to interact with their rulers peacefully. Therefore, the formula should enable the people to elect their representatives and rulers, encourage them to establish civil society organizations, prevent any majority from dominating any minority in society, and restrict the capacity of rulers to support one type of thought against another. The proposed formula calls for the following:

1. Holding periodic elections for parliamentary representatives and granting all adults the right to participate in elections, regardless of their gender, religion, and cultural affiliation.
2. Ensuring that no political party controls the parliament by limiting the maximum number of seats that any party can hold to 25% of the total.
3. Allocating parliamentary seats to the cultural and religious minorities that choose to be treated as minorities according to their size compared to society. This choice, however, should be based on a referendum where every member of the minority has the right to vote for or against this proposal.
4. Allocating 25% of the parliamentary seats to the major civil society organizations, according to their size and activities. This means expanding the concept of political plurality to become a religious, cultural, social, and professional plurality.
5. Having a constitution that dictates that the office of President be occupied by the candidate who wins the largest number of the people's votes, and that the position of Vice-President be occupied by the candidate who comes after the President in the votes. This is a new step in political thought aimed at strengthening the legitimacy of the democratic government and encouraging the ruler to be open and transparent. Such an arrangement gives the opposition the opportunity to monitor the actions of the president and prevent ideological polarity from happening and undermining the capacity of the government to function properly.

Since the people who participate in elections rarely reach 70% of the population, no political party can win an absolute majority; the winning political party therefore is more likely to get less than 35% of the people's votes. In most Third World states, only a minority vote regularly, and members of all political parties represent a small fraction of the population. Because of these facts, it is unfair to allow a party to control a parliament and claim to represent the majority of the people. With regard to the civil society organizations, their representation in parliament must be seen as a serious attempt to correct a historical error committed by the democratic system that enabled money to dominate politics, while giving private interests the opportunity to buy the loyalty of legislators and sometimes rulers as well. In fact, there is no public or private organization that combines awareness, knowledge, experience, and commitment to the public interest more than civil society organizations. In addition, these organizations are the only ones that represent all sectors of the people and the many social, cultural, religious, and economic groups. In addition, their internal elections are known for their integrity and transparency; they are also led by men and women who have the knowledge, experience, enthusiasm, and usually the honesty to serve the public interest.

A governance formula where political, social, economic, cultural, and professional plurality exists would prevent an ideologically indoctrinated leader or movement from making decisions based on their beliefs rather than on scientific facts. Decisions regarding peace and war, changing the education system or the curricula, and determining the position of the woman in society would be saved and respected. Moreover, such pluralism and the separation of powers can protect the public from media attempts to brainwash the youth and falsify their consciousness, while spreading awareness. This in turn would frustrate attempts to drag the innocent and the uneducated to take emotional positions that support ideological policies in the name of religion, nationalism, Marxism, or market capitalism. This should weaken the influence of money in the electoral process and reduce the power of lobbying.

The parliamentary system of governance used in Western democracies does not guarantee the separation of the executive, legislative, and judicial branches of government from each other. In fact, the current system leaves the three branches of government in the hands of the ruling party or coalition, sometimes for decades. Due to this fact, the parliamentary system gives the ruling party the power to monopolize the decision-making process and determine the country's future without consulting the opposition. Under such a system, the ruling party controls the legislative branch, and appoints members of the executive branch, while both branches appoint the judges and enact laws and regulations.

When people get tired of a ruling party and change it, the new party usually moves quickly to undo what its predecessor had done and put its men and ideas in the place of the old ones, remolding and controlling the three branches of government. As a consequence, the public moves from the tutelage of one party or ideological block to another, unable to free itself from being subject to the whims and wishes of a small group of people. There is no doubt, however, that the power of the ballot box causes every ruling party to be careful not to alienate the public, but it does not protect freedom of speech and often fails to prevent outlandish ideas like racism and extremism from spreading.

Therefore, there is a need for a system of governance that encourages wide participation in the political process and ensures cooperation between the different political, cultural, social, religious, and economic factions of society. Such a system is also needed to facilitate the existence of an effective opposition outside the corridors of power, activate the infomedia process, and ensure its neutrality, especially during election campaigns. For example, the parliamentary system in Britain, Germany, and Japan gives the party that controls the parliament the right to form the government or the executive branch, which makes the ministerial cabinet a miniature version of the parliament. As a consequence, the leadership of both councils would have the same ideas and views, giving the public less choices and limited options. In addition, this system makes the leaders of both councils less interested in political debate and more interested in pursuing their party goals and personal interests. The proposed folk political system is the only system of governance that overcomes this problem and opens the door for all ideas to be debated in both councils because every group is represented in the parliament.

As the folk political system separates the executive and legislative branches from each other, it entrusts the executive powers to the Council of Ministers and the President and entrusts the legislative powers to the parliament. The system also calls for the election of the prime minister from outside the ranks of the parliament while entrusting this job to the parliament, which gives the prime minister the legitimacy of being chosen by the largest elected council in society; it also gives the prime minister the right to choose members of his cabinet from outside the parliament. Though the prime minister is accountable to the president, the parliament, and the public, he does not owe his job to any party. If a political party wishes to nominate one of its members for the prime minister post, the member concerned must resign from the parliament before the voting process begins to elect the prime minister. Any deputy wishing to be a member of the cabinet must first obtain the approval of the elected prime minister, and then resign from the parliament; his seat must be declared open, and elections must be held to fill the open seat before the concerned member assumes his cabinet duties. These arrangements are meant to open the way for the appointment of ministers with knowledge and experience, develop and expand the leadership base in society, and limit the usual ideological infighting to the halls of parliament, while enabling the cabinet to focus on issues that concern the public most.

As for governance at the local level, the folk political system calls for local elections and opens the door for all strains of thought to compete; and thus it gives each political party an opportunity to apply some of its ideas on the ground. However, every elected council and official is required to follow the state's public policy as articulated by the elected legislative and executive branches of government. This means that competition at the local level would be limited to public policy implementation, with a view to improving performance and proposing new programs to exploit locally available resources and serve citizens. This requires decentralization of governance, so that national issues and local issues can be identified in a manner that allows them to be separated and integrated simultaneously.

The reason for electing the prime minister from outside the ranks of the parliament is due to the fact that thinkers and intellectuals in general tend to be concerned with public rather than local issues and focus on meeting the challenges of their times rather than interpreting and glorifying the past. In contrast, political party leaders tend to use a language that appeals to the public and has the capacity to provoke their emotions and gain their trust; such leaders often cause popular expectations to exceed available national resources, which often leads to disappointments and frustrations. So to avoid this trap and open the door to the most efficient and credible leaders to occupy some of the seats of power, the folk political system provides for the parliament to elect the Prime Minister from outside its ranks and give him/her the authority to form his cabinet from outside the parliament.

The rapid developments in various aspects of life have complicated relations between citizens and institutions on the one hand, and states and business interests across national and international borders on the other; and this has caused most parts of the world to be interconnected and interdependent. As a result, many national problems, such as human rights violations, have become global issues; and many global concerns such as environmental pollution and drug trafficking have become national issues. This in turn has weakened the sovereignty of the nation state and reduced its ability to deal with the internal and external challenges it faces. In the meantime, changes in life conditions at all levels have deepened the gaps separating the center of power in every state and the isolated regions and villages that live far away from the center, causing the institutions of the largest states to have difficulty coping with global issues, and the institutions of smaller states to have difficulty coping with local issues. All of this has weakened the ability of centralized bureaucracies to understand people's problems and deal with them efficiently.

The folk political system therefore proposes decentralization of governance to allow the central government to focus on national and global issues without neglecting local and regional ones. This means forming elected local councils and empowering them to manage people's affairs, including security, education, culture, and investment without prejudice to public policy. This will lead to dealing with most problems as they occur without delay and place the most knowledgeable and trusted individuals in a position to deal with people's concerns. A decentralized system facilitates the growth of new leaders and opens all doors for constructive competition between the regions in the fields of cultural and social activities, tourism, and economic development.

Separation of Powers

The constitutions of various democratic states call for the separation of powers, the executive power, the legislature power, and the judiciary power. There is no doubt that there is need to continue this tradition; however, term limits should be enacted and imposed on the president, the prime minister, members of parliament, and judges of the supreme court. In addition, there is need to regulate all institutions; some institutions like the mass media and social media are profit making entities and therefore should be regulated like other business concerns. All not-for-profit organizations must also be regulated because most lobbies, and many charitable foundations have goals that are not in the public interest. So to ensure that public and private organizations do not misuse the funds available to them, and be as transparent as possible, they must be regulated and supervised by special agencies.

There is a lot of talk about the media as being the fourth power in society, but this talk is limited to emphasizing the importance of the media in monitoring developments and reporting the news and analyzing public policy. However, the role of the media in influencing public opinion and setting national priorities are failing to inform the public of certain developments; in fact, failure to inform the public is more serious than fake news because it denies people the information they need to make educated decisions. The media also plays an important role in leading people to believe certain claims and accept others that sometimes undermine their interests, the public interest, as well as the human interest. For example, the American media was keen to report war crimes in Syria but ignored reporting most crimes in Yemen and Palestine, because the crimes in Syria are committed by America's adversaries, while the crimes in Yemen and Palestine are committed by America's friends with America's consent. This should be considered a violation of the human rights law.

Moreover, the largest internet and social media companies and book publishing corporations have consolidated their operations and gained control of almost every important magazine and newspaper and major entertainment organization. Consequently, a small group of transnational companies are able to control what is published in various parts of the world of news, information, and entertainment programs and promote the ideas, cultures, and rumors that the owners and sponsors of those corporations like, and suppress whatever they do not like. Today, every piece of news is subject to manipulation, distortion, falsification, or censorship. This has made it difficult for the truth to reach the people who need it most. So, to guarantee freedom of speech, the media should be subjected to the same rules, laws, and standards that apply to the executive, legislative, and judiciary branches of government. Since knowing the truth is a right that every individual in society should enjoy, all means that deal with information, publishing, and entertainment must be subject to public oversight. Otherwise, no system of governance can be just, and no just society can be established. The producer, the consumer, the worker, the student, the teacher, the professor, the jurist, the judge, the thinker, the intellectual, the inventor, the businessman, and the leader need the right information to do his job as best as he can.

Since the folk political system guarantees freedom of speech, thought, worship, assembly, and collective political and economic action, no institution should be allowed to function outside the law; freedom demands accountability; citizenship demands loyalty; and loyalty demands knowing the truth about everything that every institution does and fails to do. The folk political system believes that the president of the state should share the executive powers with the prime minister; every official elected by the people should have enough power to carry out his duties. The sharing of executive powers between the president and the prime minister prevents the formation of elite groups to monopolize power and turn the state into a corrupt, largely authoritarian system, which America is today.

Because knowledge is a human right that each person must enjoy, the state has two options; the first is to establish public book publishing companies to publish books that deal with science, medicine, drugs, and other things of importance to the average person and students and sell them at near cost; the second is to regulate all book publishing companies to force them to sell books at reasonable prices. Today the largest book publishing conglomerates are selling books at high prices, making it very difficult for students to buy and for the public to read and learn something new. But by so doing, publishers are losing a substantial segment of all societies, particularly the poor and a good portion of the cultural minorities.

The times that gave birth to the American and French democratic systems have changed drastically and irreversibly, causing the old ideas, views, and perceptions of reality and the future to be outdated. Neither the corporation, nor the media, nor the civil society organizations, nor the popular ideas are the same or even similar to what societies of the nineteenth and twentieth centuries had. This is why a new political system is needed, which the folk political system proposes. The major elements of the proposed system are as follows:

1. Direct elections for the president and members of parliament, and term limits for all.
2. The formation of a Senate whose membership includes all previous prime ministers and heads of the supreme court and speakers of the parliament, in addition to as many people as needed to make senate membership equal to one-fourth of the parliament. In case there is need to add more member, the president and the prime minister should take care of this issue.
3. If the parliament and the senate fail to reach a consensus on an issue, the parliament must have 60% of the votes to override the senate.
4. Limit the maximum number of parliamentary seats that any party can have to 25%.
5. Allocating seats in parliament to each religious and cultural minority that chooses through referendum to be treated as a minority, provided that the quota allocated to it is commensurate with its size, which should be 3% or more of the total population.

6. Allocating 25% of the seats in Parliament to the major civil society organizations, including labor and trade and consumer unions; business and finance and industrial associations; and women's, students, human rights, environmental and religious organizations, and civil rights and anti-war movements. These seats shall be distributed to these organizations according to the number of their members and their activities.
7. Each member of parliament must have at least secondary school education.
8. Each member of the cabinet must have a college degree.
9. The parliament elects the prime minister from outside its ranks; and the elected prime minister chooses his cabinet from outside the parliament as well.
10. Setting specific term limits to the president, the prime minister, members of parliament, and members of the supreme court.
11. Decentralization of governance allows for the election of local and regional councils with broad powers to manage people's daily affairs, but within the general state policy developed by the cabinet and the parliament.
12. The election system should ensure continuity and renewal by electing half of the deputies every election cycle.
13. Voting in parliament to elect the prime minister shall be by secret ballot.

Notes

1. https://news.gallup.com/poll/5392/trust-government.aspx.
2. https://povertyusa.org/facts.
3. Craig Benson, Poverty rate of children higher than national rate, lower for older populations, October 4, 2022. https://www.census.gov/library/stories/2022/10/poverty-rate-varies-by-age-groups.html.
4. Liesl Schillinger, "Snores Like Us," *Washington Post*, December 17, 1995, C1.
5. David S. Broder, *The Washington Post,* June 16, 1999, A 37.
6. Francis Fukuyama, *The End of History*, The Free Press, 1992, 134.
7. See Mohamed Rabie, *Conflict Resolution and Ethnicity*, Praeger Publishers, 1994, Chapter 10.

CHAPTER 10

The Folk Economy

Abstract This chapter presents a vision to build an efficient and just economic system able to meet the many complicated challenges of the knowledge age. However, the need for creating a visionary economic system is due to the unprecedented transformations caused by moving from the industrial age to the knowledge age. One aspect of these transformations is causing the capitalist system to lose it ability to guarantee social justice, sustain a viable middle class, ensure continued economic growth and human development, and maintain its previous competitiveness. So the need is for an economic system able to contain the deteriorating life conditions of the hundreds of millions of poor people scattered allover the world, control the income and wealth gaps separating the rich from the poor, undermine radicalism and extremism, and create the necessary conditions for world peace and economic, social, cultural, and environmental sustainability. The reason for calling the envisioned economy the "folk economy" is due to its unique social role and production relations that differ in many ways from the existing system.

Keywords Sociocultural Groups · Rainbow Society · Imagination · Solidarity · Religious Diversity · Obscene Income and Wealth Gaps · Middle Class · Corporations Consumption · Debt · Vertical Merger · Horizontal Merger

M. Rabie, *A Future Economy for All*,
https://doi.org/10.1007/978-3-031-42957-6_10

The Folk Economy is a vision to create an efficient and just economy to meet the challenges of the knowledge age. Due to the dramatic transformations the knowledge age has caused, the old capitalist system has lost its validity and capacity to perform as before and achieve the goals it is meant to achieve; the free market economy is no longer able to guarantee social justice, or sustain a viable middle class, or ensure continued economic growth and human development. So, there is need for a new economy to contain the deteriorating life conditions of the hundreds of millions of poor people in all parts of the world, control the income and wealth gaps separating the rich from the poor, undermine radicalism and extremism, and create the necessary conditions for world peace and economic, social, cultural, and environmental sustainability. The suggested folk economy is based on economic freedom but organized in ways intended to serve everyone involved in the production process, starting with the workers whose sweat enables all people to enjoy most things in life.

The reason for calling the envisioned economy the "folk economy" is due to its unique social role and production relations. The folk economy, like most other economies, is made up of countless large and small economic and financial entities, many state and private institutions, laws and regulations, and millions of workers. But unlike other economies, the components of this economy are tied to each other in ways that make them interdependent, sharing interests and a collective commitment to the general welfare of society. Due to these connections, the folk economy forms new social and economic structures and production relations that create a new society, to be called the "rainbow society." Though this society has different social classes, sociocultural groups, and forces representing the private and public sectors, all of these components form together a colorful rainbow of citizens where all groups cooperate and compete fairly to make their functions complementary and their lives pleasant and meaningful. The rainbow society recognizes that it is culturally and religiously diverse, but not racially divided, because all peoples of the world belong to one race only, the human race.

A rainbow is a collection of colors, forming together a unique body of light that makes togetherness beautiful and inspiring. If each color were to be separated from the rest, none of them would have the magic of a rainbow or the ability to inspire imagination and so are the many components of the rainbow society, while each component can stand on its own and play an independent role in society, its capacity to make a difference in societal life is limited. In contrast, being a member of a united group whose members stand in solidarity with each other makes each member more effective in influencing change, while making the life of the group more interesting and rewarding. Therefore, being together and forming one entity enables the many components of the rainbow society to shape life conditions and cultures and determine their future. If one person or an economic entity fails, a large collection of humans, economic and financial entities, private and public institutions, and civil society organizations working together cannot fail.

In the industrial society in general and the knowledge society in particular, social, cultural, and religious diversity is working today to weaken rather than strengthen the traditional bonds that tie members of each society together. In the meantime, business has divorced itself from society and its needs. In its relentless pursuit of profits, the private sector has abandoned business ethics and gained control of more than 50 percent of the world's wealth. Due to the huge social inequalities it has caused, and because of the many ways it uses money to corrupt politics and buy politicians, both large corporations and market capitalism have become beyond reform. The folk economy and the rainbow society intend to change this reality by creating new social and economic bonds to tie people together, strengthen their unity, deepen the mutuality of interests that tie them together, and lead the many social classes and cultural communities to live together a more productive and peaceful life.

A View of the Present

Economic globalization, which internationalized the major trading, financial, and investment markets, has weakened the nation state's capacity to manage its economy, while empowering the forces of the economic process at its expense. As a consequence, the nation state is no longer able to influence economic activity to ensure equal opportunity, protect the rights, and address the concerns of workers and consumers. Meanwhile, corporations' obsession with cutting expenses and maximizing profits has led them to acquire more wealth and power at the expense of the poor, the middle class, and the state. As a result, the income and wealth gaps have widened, reaching obscene levels, where the richest 1 percent of the world's population owns more than 50 percent of the global wealth. Having gained so much wealth and power, the world's super-rich seem determined to use their clout to corrupt politics, buy politicians, and change national and global policies in their favor.

In addition, allowing the world's super-rich to grab so much wealth has caused the incomes of members of the middle and the poor to remain largely stagnant, leading global demand for goods and services to slow down. This has caused the national and global economic growth rates to decline below their historic levels. A vicious cycle thus is created where a slow growing global demand for goods and services causes the global economic growth rate to slow down; and a slow growing global economy causes wages and salaries to remain largely stagnant, and stagnant wages and salaries reduce demand for goods and services, especially since the cost of living keeps rising.

On the other hand, slower economic growth rates cause states' tax revenues to be less than adequate to meet state's obligations, forcing states and consumers to borrow more and end up drowning in debt. High debt ratios in relation to consumers' incomes and GDPs is, as the 2008 financial crisis taught us, a good recipe for economic recessions. "Recent analysis from the U.K. Institute for Fiscal Studies suggests that wages will still be below 2008 levels in 2021. People work hard and companies make big profits, but employees don't have a share in the wealth they help to create,"[1] says Lynn Stuart. When workers do not get a fair share of the wealth they help create, global demand weakens causing a bad situation to get worse.

As the middle class was on its way to securing a permanent position in industrial society in the 1980s, its fortunes began to decline rapidly. The industrial economy began to shift from manufacturing goods to providing services, causing a new economy to gradually emerge, where new jobs require more education and special training which the industrial worker did not have and could not afford. But "When education fails to keep pace with technology, the result is inequality. Without the skills to stay useful as innovations arrive, workers suffer—and if enough of them fall behind, society starts to fall apart."[2] The new technical jobs which the new economy is producing today have proved to be more of a challenge to the typical industrial worker than an opportunity. Other service jobs that the new economy is creating require little or no skills and pay low wages, making them of no interest to the industrial worker. Consequently, the size of the industrial working class began to shrink gradually but systematically. For example, the American industrial workforce grew from a low of 5 percent of the labor force in 1900 to about 40 percent in 1950; however, it began thereafter to decline, reaching 25 percent in

1970 and about 15 percent in 2000, and 10 percent in 2010, and 8 percent in 2023.[3]

As markets fail to grow to meet business expectations, corporations usually move in two directions at the same time; downsizing to reduce the cost of production; and merging to consolidate operations and undermine competition. Downsizing helps companies to cut expenses and become more efficient and profitable; however, cutting expenses normally requires closing some plants, outsourcing some tasks, and reducing the labor force, which causes unemployment rates to rise. Multinational corporations often use their clout to pressure local governments to change laws and regulations in their favor, which causes the state's tax revenues to decline; and that undermines the state's capacity to fulfill its public obligations. As a result, the benefits that corporations gain from cutting expenses come at the expense of the needy workers, the poor, the schools, and the national economy. On the other hand, mergers, which could be vertical or horizontal are tools that help corporations consolidate operations, foster market positions, create oligopolies, and weaken competition.

Vertical consolidation means acquiring entities that supply parts and raw material and other products to eliminate middlemen. Horizontal merger means acquiring competitors and creating partnerships and cartels to undermine competition and tighten control over markets. By manipulating the supply of goods and services that corporations produce, they gain more power to set prices. Thus, both vertical and horizontal mergers come at the expense of workers who lose their jobs and consumers who pay higher prices for the same goods and services. Meanwhile, the absence of effective competition leads corporations to become ruthless and often heartless as well. Lack of effective competition encourages corporations to cheat consumers, avoid paying their share of taxes, and reduce wages to subsistence levels. In the process, corporations make the living conditions of the average family more difficult and less hopeful. Brexit and the election of Donald Trump can be partially attributed to the failure of the British and American governments to intervene in economic decisions to ensure fairness and equal opportunity, prevent income and wealth gaps from widening, and impoverish the poor and the middle class and damage the economy.

These unprecedented developments have created a need to rebalance the interests of the rich and powerful on the one side, and the needs of the poor and powerless on the other. This requires that nations restructure their social orders to become fair and more conducive to economic growth or create new social orders compatible with the imperatives of the new age. Failure to do so will ultimately lead to social unrest and possibly violence. States and social forces that intervened in the past need to intervene again to promote economic growth and ensure that workers get a fair share of the fruits of their sweat.

Driven by greed and lust for power, the rich and super-rich have shown little regard for community life, and almost no interest in the tragic life conditions of the world's poor. Nevertheless, the poor and powerless, despite their miserable living conditions, are not expected to revolt soon to reclaim their rights and force the creation of just social orders. During eras of civilizational change and historical discontinuities, ordinary people get confused, lose their sense of direction, and become conservative seeking hope in religious promises and traditional values that discourage change, dampen expectations, and encourage contentment.

The 2008 financial crisis has proven that market capitalism is neither able to keep the world economy growing, prevent financial crises and economic recessions from occurring, nor create jobs for the unemployed and most high school graduates. In fact, market capitalism and the new technological innovations and gadgets that are being developed have become a force of disruption, spreading chaos and fear, and causing confusion and loss of direction. In addition, they are creating a large and growing number of people whose skills are being outdated daily; and influencing cultures in ways that are more negative than positive. People obsessed with smart phones, for example, have become more inclined to use the printed word instead of the spoken one, causing them to become less social and more individualistic.

Since profits have become the organizing principle of business organizations, economic considerations rather than political or social ones guide the economic process today and shape its relationships to the other processes. Due to the power it has gained since the 1980s, the economic process is able to manipulate political actors and strengthen its capacity to function freely. On the other hand, the political process, unwilling to surrender its traditional authority, is struggling to impose its will on a powerful economic process, as it loses its power to provide adequate protection for workers and consumers, the needy, and the environment. While some states like China are still able to control economic decisions; states like Germany and France are only able to influence business decisions; while other states like the United States and Britain seem to have lost their capacities to align corporate interests with the national interest.

In the new knowledge age, due primarily to the information and telecommunications revolutions, social change has become a dynamic process of transformation that has no end in sight. Since the services of the twin revolutions are in need everywhere, their impact stretches beyond all political borders; it involves all peoples, cultures, and societies, and because the institutions through which these revolutions function are controlled by the rich, the ideas and actions of the rich influence the lives of all individuals, groups, nations, and states. In the wake of the collapse of communism and the end of the Cold War, the rich began to use their power to gain control of the major economic activities and financial and media organizations. To consolidate their powers, the world's rich are competing less and cooperating more with each other, while keeping global conflict manageable and change sustainable, because conflict and change are tools to enhance wealth and power.

I believe that Marxism and the socialist system it built before 1990 was the last serious attempt launched by politics to control economics. The collapse of the Soviet Union on the one hand, and China's shift to capitalism on the other, put an end to the Marxist system, which the failure of socialism to empower the industrial working class precipitated. As a consequence, the forces of the economic process won their last battle against politics. The triumph of Donald Trump in 2016 is a significant step toward consolidating the powers of the economic process to control the forces of the political process and subordinate them to its will. Nevertheless, it is not easy for the forces of the economic process to win their vicious war against the vanquished and impoverished masses of the world. Therefore, the struggle for freedom, equal opportunity, and social justice is expected to continue and make conflict and war and the suffering of children a never-ending human tragedy.

Economy and the Knowledge Age

Technologies to enhance our ability to deal with every aspect of life are being developed at the speed of light. Countless individuals and groups residing in hundreds of towns and villages across the world, working through thousands of organizations with varied, often contradictory goals, are participating in this unique process. As a result, a world in transition is slowly emerging, where many forces are instigating change and causing social transformations of immense proportions and consequences. It is estimated that the last 30 years of the twentieth century had witnessed "tenfold increase in communications by electronic means and tenfold reduction in person-to person contact,"[4] causing writing letters and traveling long distances to discuss issues of mutual concern to be vastly reduced. Since the pace of change is accelerating, it has caused our world to become a world in a constant state of transition.

A world in transition describes a society in which no stable situations exist or could exist. Change in such societies moves in all directions, works at all levels, and affects all peoples and relationships at the same time, and as it moves change produces winners and losers, with both having different social and cultural backgrounds, as well as needs and interests. Because of this complexity and dynamism, no particular trend of change can be defined with clarity and accepted as desirable or opposed as undesirable, causing future planning for social, economic, and political change to become more complicated and challenging than ever before.

In the meantime, knowledge workers have become capitalists possessing valuable social capital consisting of specialized skills and positive attitudes that can be invested in several ways, in several places. Since knowledge frees people from need, knowledge workers have become freer and thus less dependent on their states, communities, or families; and as a consequence, they share little collective memories with others, and are committed to no particular ideology. Their primary interest is to succeed, make the best use of whatever knowledge they may have, and get the most for it. As a result, most knowledge workers have become nomads wandering from one place to another, from one organization to another and from one country to another to advance technically and succeed materially.

Due to the increasing life complexity in the knowledge age, law has become more complicated but less able to keep pace with change, leaving big loopholes to be exploited by the rich and powerful people, as well as criminals. As a result, money is allowed to buy justice, making the law largely a tool to serve the interests of the powerful and protect the privileges of the rich. On the other hand, as the rich and powerful gain more freedom, they feel that they have many rights and few obligations, while the poor and weak have many obligations and few rights. A critical look at America today will reveal that neither equality of opportunity, nor equality of rights nor equality of citizenship exist; it may be part of the law, but not part of the culture of the majority of White Americans.

In traditional agricultural society, leadership is largely authoritarian, and domination is accepted by farmers, legitimized by religion or traditions, and exercised by coercion. In industrial society, authority is largely democratic; it is legitimized by direct elections and exercised by the courts and state institutions. In the emerging knowledge society, authority has become weak and formless and hard to identify its source; it is legitimized by elite consensus, exercised by scattered centers of political, economic, and military power and special interest groups, and facilitated by media manipulation of the masses and the subjugation of every human feeling and need and desire to profits.

The industrial society was the only society in history that could and did produce a credible middle class. The tribal society had only one class, the agricultural society has two classes, and the knowledge society is divided more into sociocultural groups than socioeconomic classes; therefore, the knowledge society is neither able to sustain the middle class it inherited from the industrial society nor produce a new one. The appearance of the middle class, therefore, must be considered an aberration in social history. Since history never repeats itself, we need to adjust our assumptions to reflect this fact and deal with it rationally. Even the industrializing Asian nations are not expected to emulate the Western experience and produce middle classes capable of influencing social change in their favor. People who have middle-class incomes in a knowledge society are unable to form a class, because the nature of their work and their global associations deny them the opportunity to develop a class consciousness; one of the major requirements for forming a social class.

The new economy, which began to take shape in the mid-1990s, is knowledge-based and service-oriented. Since the association of wealth with knowledge is strong and getting stronger, it seems that any possibility that the industrial working class will ever recapture its past glory has vanished under the current economic system; its chance of growing again and regaining enough confidence and class consciousness to cause social change in its favor are near zero. Whoever gets enough knowledge and/or wealth today, even if his roots are in the industrial working class, is destined to have different associations and values, and to entertain different dreams. In addition, the Western mass media, and particularly the American media, are constantly bombarding members of the poor and middle classes with information and images meant to convince them to accept the unacceptable, while the forces of religious fundamentalism are working hard to convince them to accept their lot in life and be content.

The experience of industrial societies since the 1980s suggests that as the rich get richer and more powerful, the middle class shrinks in size and influence, and the poor get poorer and more desperate, and the national economy slows down. In fact, the American experience has demonstrated that as the rich get richer, business creation declines and reduces the number of opportunities available to the public. "In America the rate of business creation has declined since the late 1970s. In some recent years more companies died than were born."[5] Though this development is largely due to business mergers, it means that empowering the rich and powerful causes inequalities to widen, hurts the middle class and the poor, and undermines the state's capacity to grow its economy and care for its citizens. To stop this rather destructive process, the state needs to intervene, assume an active role in promoting economic growth and directing investment to serve the common good; the state must also ensure that the fruits of economic growth are fairly distributed among all participants in the economy.

In the coming 15–20 years, I expect the manufacturing jobs in the world to decline by 50% or more due to automation and the advancements in robot technology and artificial intelligence. Since the industrial workers represent the core of the traditional middle class, the size of the middle class, as a result, is expected to shrink further, while the ranks of the poor are expected to grow, causing the world economy to slow down. Industrial workers are so important to forming and sustaining a credible middle class because of their ability to develop a class consciousness which most people earning middle class incomes today are unable to do. A new set of regulations is therefore needed to facilitate the building of an alternative social class; and that can only be achieved by bringing industrial workers and blue-collar employees and owners of small businesses together. The arrangements outlined in the following section are designed to tie these groups of people together through stock ownership in the companies they work for and deal with, creating shared interests and class consciousness; otherwise, no middle class will survive the transformation of the knowledge age, and whoever earns a middle-class income will become a middle person helping the rich and powerful to control, dominate, and exploit everyone else.

Building a Folk Economy

To build the desired folk economy, we offer a plan to reduce the cost of production, improve economic productivity and competitiveness, restore corporate social responsibility, provide universal health care and free education for all citizens, revitalize the middle class, and above all, give each member of society the opportunity to own a share in the national economy. While a solid middle class is essential to stimulating national economies and improving productivity and sustaining democracy, helping members of society to own a share of their economy and participate in its management guarantees fairness and equal opportunity. The proposed plan is as follows:

First, the state should enact laws that require all public corporations to pay 25% of their employees' salaries in company stock, using the stock market to determine the price of shares at the closing of the stock market on the day of each pay period. This action is intended to help companies reduce the cost of production, not by resorting to mergers, outsourcing, closing certain plants, and firing employees, but by helping employees become shareholders. Since employees are accustomed to getting paid in cash, the stock payment should be introduced gradually over two years. It is further suggested that employees be required to hold such shares for at least two years before they could sell any portion of them; this condition should also be introduced gradually. Nevertheless, it is suggested that the policy be implemented from day one in regard to new employees. In addition, it is suggested that employees should not pay taxes on the money they use to purchase company stock; instead, they should pay income taxes on the money they receive whenever they sell any of the shares they own.

After two years, almost every employee will have 25% of his and her annual salary invested in his and her company, causing an active and rather stable block of shareholders to gradually evolve. Creating such a block of shareholders that care about the financial situation of their companies and how they are managed is badly needed to motivate employees to become more innovative and productive and empower them to influence the compensation packages of corporations' managers and regulate the bonuses managers grant themselves every year.

Claims that stockholders bear responsibility for the obscene management salaries and bonuses are either misplaced or dishonest. Most buyers and sellers in the stock markets these days are not investors in the traditional sense; they do not buy and wait for dividends at the end of each year. Instead, they tend to make their decisions to buy, hold, and sell on the basis of the actual and projected prices of the shares they trade. In fact, trading in the US stock markets has become a new form of gambling in a highly dynamic, vastly unpredictable casino. But unlike Las Vegas casinos, this one is subject to manipulation by major shareholders and traders. Since most small investors trust the buying and selling of shares to financial companies and advisors, ownership in most traded shares changes hands every second. Thus creating a solid and rather permanent block of invested stockholders is probably the only way to give shareholders a voice in managing the corporations they work for and partially own. On the other hand, helping employees build assets and become more involved in the management of the corporations they work for is the right way to foster corporate loyalty, encourage innovations, improve labor productivity, and strengthen the middle class. In fact, the creation of a fairly large and active group of shareholders is the only way to create an empowered social class to replace the disappearing traditional middle class.

The implementation of this proposal would reduce the cost of production to corporations immediately; and vastly limit the need to borrow from banks; it will also give corporations a stream of cash to upgrade equipment, expand operations, and repay outstanding loans, and thus reduce the need to borrow money. Corporations that worry about diluting share prices or stock ownership by issuing new shares every pay period can use a portion of the saved money to buy back some of their stock. Meanwhile, employees will be able to get the cash they may need by selling some of the shares they own; and this would reduce workers' need to borrow from lenders at high interest rates to meet emergencies. Since stocks tend to appreciate rather than depreciate over the long run, most employees are likely to make more money due to this proposal. The option to buy shares should also be offered to persons and entities that deal with each company, like suppliers of parts and services.

The application of this policy should help all corporations become more competitive, selling more at home and possibly abroad; and by selling more, more jobs would be created. In the meantime, workers will be empowered and feel secure having saved for their retirement, children's education, and emergencies, and economies will be invigorated, causing the state's revenues from taxes to rise. Helping workers and employees feel secure and creating more jobs causes domestic markets to grow while reducing most companies' dependence on exports to foreign markets.

A policy to enable employees to become stockholders and encourage them to build equity in the companies they work for is probably the only feasible way to put industrial and blue-collar workers on the right path to middle-class status; it will also lead workers to become aware of their rights and more appreciative of the benefits of saving and investing. I believe that most corporations, after seeing the positive impact of such a plan on the cost of production, labor productivity, competitiveness, and innovation, would welcome it and adopt it. Nevertheless, as far as all new corporations are concerned, this policy should become the law and therefore should be implemented from day one; however, established corporations should be allowed to implement the plan over a 5- to 7-year period to give them the time to change their policies and adapt their management systems.

Second, the folk economy calls for corporations to create special funds to loan money to their employees in need at slightly lower rates than the market rates, using employees' shares as collateral. Such funds will deepen employees' loyalty to their companies and respect for their managers, causing each party to feel more appreciated and comfortable dealing with the other. With loyalty and respect reinforced, employee productivity increases and dedication to serving the company becomes the norm rather than the exception. Thus a community whose members are tied to each other by interests and mutual respect forms and prospers.

I believe that these two modest proposals are able to achieve by themselves some of the most desired but hard-to-accomplish social and economic objectives:

1. Reducing the cost of production immediately and substantially.
2. Improving the quality of products and raising the competitiveness of national companies.
3. Creating a clear path to building a solid and growing middle class of workers and employees tied to each other and to a productive economic process.
4. Restoring corporate social responsibility and guaranteeing accountability, while making it hard for corporations to ignore business ethics.
5. Raising labor productivity and encouraging innovation and creativity; and

6. Creating new production relations that strengthen worker to worker bonds; deepen mutual interests and obligations that tie workers to corporations; raise the level of cooperation and trust between workers and management; and strengthen the commitment of both workers and corporations to their nations and the welfare of their peoples.

Third, the folk economy also calls for enacting new laws to give the employees of each company priority to buy their company in case the management decides to move production operations to a foreign country or stop operations or offer the company or some of its operations for sale. This policy alone would substantially slow down mergers and acquisitions, sustain competition, and create many labor-owned and managed companies. To minimize the risk associated with such transactions, the state should establish a special agency to evaluate the viability and future prospects of companies on sale or about to go out of business. Since employees of most companies do not have enough money to buy most companies offered for sale, the state should establish a national investment bank to partner with employees and share with them the probable risks involved and possible profits expected.

Fourth, the establishment of a national investment bank (NIB) to provide venture capital to innovators and young entrepreneurs with creative ideas and to finance the development of new products, rehabilitate old industries, and help finance labor-owned enterprises. In fact, most economies in the world are in need of new entrepreneurs, because most managers and entrepreneurs of today are driven by greed and lust for money and power. In the process of chasing money and power, the current managers and entrepreneurs lost whatever business ethics they may have had in the past, which led them to become parasites living on sucking the blood of the people close to them. In addition, corporations that manipulate consumers and cheat them are, unconsciously, training a new generation of managers who are accustomed to manipulating and cheating their customers. This has made the future of business ethics grow bleaker day after day, while lowering economic growth rates and making the economy subject to recurring episodes of inflation and recessions.

The establishment of a national investment bank is indispensable for raising economic growth rates, for sustaining a viable manufacturing sector and creating jobs for high school and university graduates, and for building a creative and innovative young entrepreneurial class. Investment capital, as the experience of the last two decades has demonstrated, has no identity, religion, ideology, or cause, except making money. Capital is a strange creature; it is willing to do business with anyone, at any time, in any place, as long as business deals promise good returns. For example, the US media reported that the largest 500 American corporations earn more than 50% of their profits from overseas operations. General Electric made $14.2 billion in profits in 2010, of which only $5.1 billion were made in the United States; the rest, which amounts to 60% of the profits, were made overseas. Therefore, no efforts can sustain a dynamic industrial economy without public investment.

As profits from foreign operations increased, large Western corporations became less inclined to invest in their home countries, and more interested in establishing production operations in other states. As a result, most traditional industrial economies slowed down, societies lost jobs, except for low-paying service jobs, consequently, the size of the middle classes shrank. Since national corporations working in foreign countries are able to export their products to their home states, the incentive to train domestic workers and upgrade their skills has diminished. In fact, large corporations and investment banks have found a new business model to increase their profits without having to hire more workers or take the usual risks. The model is based on reducing payrolls by reducing the size of the workforce, paying new employees less than what they pay the old ones, and investing overseas where wages are low, productivity is good, and markets are growing.

To be effective, the proposed National Investment Bank should be well capitalized and managed by an independent and highly qualified board of directors. Private capital should be encouraged to participate in capitalizing NIB; however, the state should maintain majority ownership in NIB at all times. Projects initiated or sponsored or aided by NIB should be opened to the private sector to invest in and participate in their management; nevertheless, NIB should keep majority ownership in each enterprise until it becomes profitable and goes public. All successful enterprises should be taken public, and all shares owned by NIB should be sold within 2–3 years of being profitable. As such, NIB will serve as an institution committed to economic growth and diversification, and to creating new enterprises that open new venues for the private sector to benefit from. In addition, NIB will facilitate the creation of a new entrepreneurial class that appreciates the state and public service. Nevertheless, workers and employees of all enterprises should continue to receive 25% of their salaries in stock.

No industrial nation that has benefited substantially from globalization, including Japan, South Korea, and China has done so without an industrial policy that encourages investment in new industries, finances research and development activities, and protects national industries directly or indirectly. If NIB were to be structured along the suggested lines, it would become an engine of economic growth and an asset to the nation; it would lead by example and distribute whatever profits it generates among all individual and corporate participants; it would also achieve the following goals:

1. Help create hundreds or thousands of small enterprises year after year.
2. Keep national talent at home and thus slow down the brain drain process.
3. Save thousands of small companies from bankruptcy year after year.
4. Facilitate the emergence of a new entrepreneurial class that owes its existence and good fortunes to the state and society.
5. Slow down mergers, acquisitions, and outsourcing; and thus discourage national corporations from moving production operations to foreign countries.
6. Reduce the vulnerability of national economies to the ups and downs of the global economy, because small enterprises rely primarily on domestic markets; and
7. Provide the state with new sources of income, causing the general tax rates to remain reasonable.

Fifth, the establishment of technical training institutes to train a new generation of workers able to excel in two professions and arm them with the right attitudes. The state should also develop high-quality programs for all high school graduates to ensure that no one is left without adequate skills. In addition, training programs should be updated continuously to ensure that employees do not fall behind technological change that does not stop evolving. Everyone should realize that the only thing that does not change is change itself; everything else keeps changing. "Today robotics and artificial intelligence call for another education revolution. This time, however, working lives are so lengthy and fast changing that simply cramming more schooling at the start is not enough. People must be able to acquire new skills throughout their careers. Unfortunately, the lifelong learning that exists today mainly benefits high achievers—and is therefore more likely to exacerbate inequality. If 21st-century economies are not to create a massive underclass, policymakers urgently need to work out how to help all their citizens learn while they earn."[6] As Frank A. Clack said: "The more you learn, the more you earn"; and as I say: "The more you read, the more you succeed."

While countries of Western Europe in general, and Germany in particular, have done a good job training their young to find work in a changing world, the United States has failed to do so; the majority of vocational training schools in America are private ones; many were found to be more interested in making money than in caring for the young and the disadvantage to train them how to succeed in life. "Historically, middle schools and high schools have offered vocational courses such as home economics, wood and metal shop, typing, business courses, drafting, construction, and auto repair. However, for a number of reasons, many schools have cut those programs. Some schools no longer have the funding to support these programs, and schools have since put more emphasis on academics for all students."[7]

As for the Third World states, vocational training is in a bad shape; this is due to several reasons. In countries where the predominant culture has its roots in the tribal society, people tend to look down on menial work, that is work that requires the use of hands to perform, such as tasks related to agriculture, home building, and car repair; most Arab and African societies fall in this category. In most Asian countries, the state did not give enough attention to vocational training because it lacks both the awareness and the financial and technical resources. However, academic education was given priority to boost the national spirit and train new leaders. However, the German experience following the First World War proves that vocational training and technical education is the foundation for building industries and nations and competitive economies. Building good institutions and systems is not enough to keep a society making progress, maintaining the institutions and systems in good working conditions is more important, particularly in the long run. Arab universities that were built before the 1970s were good and competitive, however all such universities have failed to stay competitive; most of them have in fact deteriorated to the point of becoming hardly relevant.

Under the old capitalist system, corporations used to hire workers and train them to do the work that manufacturing required. Due to the substantial investments corporations had to make in their employees, they used to take care of them and often keep them until retirement. Today, corporations are building production facilities wherever labor is cheap and skilled and have the right attitudes; and therefore corporations are no longer interested in spending money training new workers they are unlikely to keep them for long. Since industrial and knowledge jobs are chasing qualified labor wherever it exists, a need has been created in every country to train all willing high school graduates to have two skills. People with more than one skill are more likely to find jobs easily; and have an easier time avoiding unemployment during difficult times. While many nations in the West and East have outstanding universities capable of training knowledge workers, most developing nations do not have good technical institutes to train workers for the knowledge economy. I believe that every person has special talents that can be developed; and developed talents make people more productive, more positive, more responsible, more hopeful, and thus better citizens.

Sixth, states need to have progressive tax codes that distribute the tax load among all citizens fairly. Higher rates of taxes imposed on the rich and large corporations should be viewed as ways to guarantee fairness, not to punish anyone for making money. When rich individuals and corporations pay higher income taxes, they would be in fact sharing a small portion of their excessive incomes and profits with their workers whose sweat had helped them become rich. The rich also have more to lose if the security of their country is compromised or the national debt skyrockets or the social situation worsens due to widespread poverty, unemployment, or economic stagnation. So, social fairness, good economics, and social peace dictate that tax laws should be progressive.

Notes

1. Lynn Stuart Parramore, *Capitalism in the Time of Trump*? AlterNet, December 9, 2016. www.alternet.org/economy/capitalism-time-trump?akid=14990.245927.UVGPgw&rd=1&src=newsletter106858&t=6
2. Equipping people to stay ahead of technological change, *The Economist*, January 14, 2017.

3. Number of employees in the United States in May 2023, by industry. https://www.statista.com/statistics/978479/number-employees-united-states-industry/
4. The Economist, Management theory is becoming a compendium of dead ideas, December 17, 2016.
5. Equipping people to stay ahead of technological change, *The Economist*, January 14, 2017.
6. Vocational education in the United States; *Wikipedia*.
7. Ibid, https://en.wikipedia.org/wiki/Vocational_education_in_the_United_States

CHAPTER 11

Inventing a new Educational System

Abstract This chapter presents a totally new idea to create an educational system capable of facing the many challenges of the knowledge age while meeting the needs of tomorrow's societies, particularly the young men and women who are forced to transform their attitudes and living conditions as times change. While societal change was hardly noticeable during the agricultural age, it accelerated gradually during the industrial age, and became extremely hard to follow during the current knowledge age. Due to this change, a need was created for building an unconventional education system with a built-in capacity to transform itself to maintain creativity and adaptability to changing times, new scientific facts, and unprecedented technological innovations. The transition from one civilization to another creates a new society, having its unique culture, economy, and social, political, and economic structures. All of which dictate that people change their views, attitudes, and patterns of life.

Keywords Internet · Communication · Information · Artificial Intelligence · Archeological Discoveries · Evolving · Schools · Universities · Sunrise System · Cultural Illiteracy · Cultural Ghettos

Ten years ago, I published a book to explain the development of human societies, and thus the making of human history; Global Economic and

M. Rabie, *A Future Economy for All*,
https://doi.org/10.1007/978-3-031-42957-6_11

Cultural Transformation: the Making of History; (Palgrave Macmillan 2013). According to this theory, human societies never stopped changing and evolving; at the beginning change was very slow, but it accelerated with the passing of time. However, the tribal age lasted about 30 thousand years without noticeable social change or cultural transformation; it lived on the hunting of animals and the collection of wild plants and fruits. Throughout that period, the tribe was the unit of society and the entire society because the state did not exist then. But during the last two thousand years of being the dominant pattern of life, the tribal society entered a new phase that witnessed important change. The tribal man was able to domesticate several animals including the horse, camel, elephant, donkey, goat, dog, chicken, and others. These animals allowed tribes to become semi-settled, which gave the tribal woman the opportunity to discover the life cycle of plants and develop the art of agriculture. Though tribal societies still exist today in many parts of the world, the traditional tribal way of life has disappeared. The transition from grazing and hunting to planting the land took about three thousand years to complete and give birth to the agricultural age and its fundamentally different pattern of life, causing all aspects of life to be transformed, while enabling humanity to take its first step toward civilization.

In the middle of the fifteenth century, the agricultural society began to change systematically and shift from concentrating on planting the land and living on its products to producing manufactured goods and machines and create services, and developing the scientific way of thinking, causing agriculture itself to be transformed into an industry. In the second half of the eighteenth century, industry became the dominant pattern of life in most European states and America, causing the agricultural age to end and pave the way for the industrial age to dominate societal life in general. This means that the transition from the agricultural age to the industrial age took about 300 years only; one-tenth of the time that the tribal society needed to be transformed from being tribal to becoming agricultural.

In the early 1990s, a new wave of change and transformation appeared; the communications and information revolutions and the Internet revolutionized the way we communicate with one another and view the world and our place in it. As a result, the industrial society started evolving fast and becoming a knowledge society that focused more on producing services than on manufactured goods and related products. Since the transition from the tribal to the agricultural age needed about 3,000 years to be completed, and the transition from the agricultural to the industrial age needed about 300 years to be completed, I concluded that the transition from the industrial to the knowledge age would take about 30 years only, ending around 2025.

Since every transitional period takes about one-tenth the time which the previous one needed to be completed, the new transition that will follow the knowledge age will need about three years only. This means that we will be living from now on in a continuous state of transition that cannot be stopped or even give us enough time to fully understand it and describe its characteristics. We need to realize that as society goes through a transitional period, every aspect of its life changes, causing a new society with its own culture and economy to be created that has its own social, economic, and political structures that differ fundamentally from the previous ones. For example, the technology that gave us the iPhone during the early years of the knowledge age gave us the technology that created social media and artificial intelligence and ways to manipulate our genes and view our world, its past and future. Archeological advancements have enabled us to read the past more accurately than ever and discover the fallacies of religious tales and thus change our understanding of the past. With this knowledge, honest archeologists have helped us overcome ideology and its countless ideological misunderstandings and view the past differently; they also encouraged us to work together and try to create a new, more realistic, and human world for all.

Since education is the system through which we learn new things, discover new facts, create new ideas, produce new knowledge, and transform our societies and outlook, the education system needs to be transformed. When thinking about developing a modern educational system, we must first think about the rules that must govern that system, and these can only be determined if the objectives which the society concerned seeks to achieve are identified and adopted. However, most people in charge of educational systems in most parts of the world are often chosen on the basis of their past experiences accumulated during their involvement in education; however, this experience tends to be governed by outdated traditions and values. As a result, old experiences have become largely irrelevant and useless; it is knowledge and experience whose time had come and gone and will not come back again, just like the tribal and agricultural experiences and the knowledge they produced.

Education reform processes have therefore to start by asking questions not about the past, but about what we expect to happen in the future and how to influence the direction of future change to meet our needs and achieve our objectives. Since change is unstoppable, and all mistakes we made in the past and still making cannot be reversed, we need to be careful and thoughtful in constructing new education systems, knowing in advance that these systems must be viewed as evolving systems that require continuous attention to meet the challenges of the times we pass through on our way to the unknown. This means that we must realize that no change is going to be permanent, and no state of living will endure for a long time.

The following is a proposal to build a new education system of study in primary, middle, and secondary schools; the system separates knowledge in general and science in particular from the age of students, giving science precedence over other topics. The system allows older students to study subjects that new students study and allows younger students to study subjects that older students study. This process creates an age difference between the young and old students that ranges from one to three years. This would transcend age sensitivities and establish relationships based on competence, need, cooperation, desire, mutual respect, and learning from the other. The proposed system, to be called the "**Sunrise System**," divides the twelve-year primary, middle, and secondary levels into three stages, each one lasting four years.

This system, being creative, innovative, and dynamic, suggests that the first four years, or the first educational stage should focus on learning languages, mathematics and various computer uses, and skills that every human being needs to function rationally in a turbulent world. In addition, students will study the geography and history of their countries and the population makeup of their societies, as well as the aspects of their old and current cultures. Languages consist mainly of two languages: a universal language and a national-regional language. The first language is English because there is no other language comparable to English in terms of ease to learn and use, richness of knowledge, and availability of references. In fact, information says that the percentage of scientific research published in English is about 75% of what is published in the world, in addition to being the language of tourism and banking everywhere. The second language is the language used in the homeland and the region surrounding it, where most visits, commercial and financial transactions, and the import and export of goods take place. It is also advisable to offer students an opportunity to study a third language that appeals to them. As for mathematics, every person needs to be able to complete simple financial and commercial transactions, regardless of his age. Skills should also include using computers to prepare students at an early age to study social, management, and natural sciences during the following two educational stages.

In the second stage, which also lasts four years, the focus will be on social sciences of all kinds, each student will have the right to choose five subjects each year, with a focus on critical thinking, classroom discussion, and research based on analysis. Each student will be required to prepare two research papers on each of the subjects he chooses to study. In an attempt to figure out how many subjects could be categorized under the heading of social sciences, I found more than forty headlines, some of which are subheadings of the major ones. The main titles of these sciences include sociology, anthropology, economics, democracy, capitalism, political science, systems of government, conflict resolution, history of the world, cultures, religions, comparative religions, philosophy, psychology, history of colonialism, environmental sciences, poverty, education, leadership, arts, media, village culture, city culture, refugee camps culture, migrant culture, women and society, women rights, thought and intellectualism, faith and ideology, methods of scientific research, and literature that includes poetry, novels, and the arts such as painting, music, dance, acting, and popular sports.

In addition, two fields I invented about 15 years ago, "cultural ghettos" and "cultural illiteracy" need to be developed further and added to the curricula of each system. While cultural illiteracy is widespread in all countries, especially in the developing ones, cultural ghettos are spreading like wildfire everywhere, they undermine human interactions and social relations, especially between the young and old people, intensify cultural illiteracy, deepen ignorance and often arrogance as well, increase discrimination and racism, and endanger our humanity. Therefore, cultural illiteracy and cultural ghettoes should be developed into full topics to expose their nature, how they evolved, what role they play in society, and explain their impact on individual and collective life of society.

In the last four years of secondary school, emphasis is placed on natural sciences, with special attention to biology, physics, chemistry, space sciences, marine sciences, professional sciences such as medicine, engineering, management, finance, banking, financial markets, and scientific theories such as the relativity and the creationist theories, international security systems, electronic currency, artificial intelligence, the future of work, the law and its societal role, crime and punishment, health care systems, and international organizations and their role in maintaining global security, promoting peace, and protecting our environment. Despite the many things I have mentioned in this field, I am sure that other educators interested in the state of education in the world will add more to what I have mentioned here and crystallize my ideas within a general institutional framework. That should create a sociocultural movement led by school administrators and university professors and global intellectuals to build a new education system that can surpass most if not all education systems in various countries of the world.

The **Sunrise System** also suggests that all schools be adopted by the universities in each country and allow students of the third stage to visit their mother universities and attend classes they choose and participate in class discussions. In addition, students of all stages should be allowed to attend public lectures and participate in university trips and folk activities. As mentioned earlier, all students have the right to go back and study whatever they missed studying and go forward to learn more of what interests them most. As a result, by the time students of the third stage graduate, they would have enough exposure to all fields of study and gained adequate amount of knowledge to decide what to study at university. Since specializations change continuously and evolve producing the need to handle new jobs and manage changing situations, both high school and college graduates should be able to go back to their schools and universities and update their information and learn more about the requirements that qualify them for the new opportunities that are expected to continue opening without interruption.

For the **Sunrise System** to be developed and adopted by nations to serve their interests, all states need to make education free of fees and open to all students without restrictions. Universal healthcare and good education are not only human right issues, but also the path to a bright, more promising future for individuals and nations alike. In addition, there is a need for identifying, analyzing, and dealing with the cultural illiteracy issue; however, this serious issue and how to deal with will be discussed in detail in the following chapter.

CHAPTER 12

Education and Healthcare

Abstract This chapter seeks to give its readers an idea about the healthcare crisis in some countries and explain how important healthcare is to respect the dignity of man and his human rights, and helping him to enjoy a better, healthy pattern of life. It also intends to give an idea about the importance of good education in creating awareness of where we are in our development as human beings and why we continue to misunderstand each other and have conflict. Based on this, the chapter provides some ideas to improve the delivery systems of both education and healthcare. In so doing, the purpose stays the same: creating a better future for all peoples of our mother earth.

Keywords Healthcare · Insurance companies · World Health Organization · World Bank · Physicians · Human rights · Education · Students · Diploma · Schools · Universities · Tsunami · Third World · Traditional wisdom · Liberating · Community

This chapter intends to give an idea about the healthcare crisis in some countries and explain how important healthcare is to respect the dignity of man and his human rights. It also intends to give an idea about the importance of good education in creating awareness of where we are in our development as human beings and why we continue to misunderstand

M. Rabie, *A Future Economy for All*,
https://doi.org/10.1007/978-3-031-42957-6_12

each other and have conflict. Based on this, I shall provide some ideas to improve the delivery systems of both education and healthcare, and in so doing, the purpose stays the same: creating a better future for all peoples of our mother earth.

Education is universally acknowledged as a basic human right that every person in the world should enjoy; and it is the duty of the state to provide. In contrast, healthcare is not universally acknowledged as a basic human right; and therefore probably over two billion people in the world have no healthcare insurance coverage. In the United States there are more than 30 million Americans without health insurance, most of whom are poor; and during the first two years of Donald Trump's presidency, the number of the uninsured increased by 3.2 million. This happened despite the fact that the economy has continued to grow at a robust rate, and the rate of unemployment has declined to historic lows. In addition, there are 41 million Americans who have inadequate health insurance, according to the Commonwealth Fund.[1]

Education

History seems to suggest that human progress toward higher levels of economic, social, cultural, and scientific achievements has four basic requirements: sociocultural transformation, technological development, accumulation of knowledge, and man's relentless struggle for freedom; all of which cannot be accomplished without the right education that informs and guides people, and the social awareness it creates and fosters in society.

"Education is the primary vehicle through which societies produce knowledge and transmit it from one generation to another, preserve certain values and traditions and transform others, and introduce change in the form of new ideas, systems, and ways of thinking. It is through education that people become more socially and politically aware and develop a capacity to acquire knowledge and use it to improve the quality of their lives. But for education to instigate the desired transformations, it has to have the right institutions, teach the right knowledge, and help students acquire the right attitudes and appreciate the value of work, time, and life,"[2] says Mohamed Rabie.

But for education to instigate the desired sociocultural transformations and produce the know-how needed to achieve material, cultural, and scientific progress, it has to come with other things, most important among them are the right knowledge, the right attitudes, and the right training. Education that fails to instill in students the right attitudes and equip them with the proper training and expose them to the right information and scientific facts can create obstacles to change that hinder rather than facilitate sociocultural transformation and scientific and technological progress.

College students who regard getting good education as the primary objective of their college life are more likely to acquire the right knowledge and attitudes and succeed in life. In contrast, students who consider getting a college diploma the primary objective of attending university, are likely to acquire little knowledge without acquiring the right attitudes; as a consequence, they are more likely to become social liabilities rather than social assets. Students who fail to get involved in university life and nonacademic activities and shy away from seeking new knowledge may get a diploma at the end of their college life, but they are more likely to fail the test of life. While it is the responsibility of the university to provide students with the right education and training to think critically and creatively and face life challenges with courage; it is the responsibility of schools and homes to provide students with the right attitudes toward learning and living healthy and productive lives.

"Formal education, especially among people for whom it is rare or recent, often creates feelings of entitlement to rewards and exemptions from many kinds of work,"[3] says David Landes. In addition, expanding education where education is recent creates popular expectations that the state is often unable to meet, even rich states like Algeria and Venezuela. When education comes without the right attitudes, unmet expectations often cause social and political unrest that complicates rather than facilitates societal development. Nevertheless, faced with high illiteracy rates, most developing states were forced to provide low-quality education and create bloated bureaucracies to absorb graduates.

Low-quality education usually nurtures certain attitudes that weaken prospects for raising labor productivity and facilitating sociocultural transformation. Third World bureaucrats tend to humiliate rather than respect the people they are supposed to serve, exploit rather than assist the poor and powerless, resist rather than encourage reform, and detest rather than welcome creativity and initiative. Education that comes with negative attitudes, such as despising menial work and having no appreciation for work and time, is likely to reduce labor productivity rather than increase it. In addition, it is hard to teach new skills to students with negative attitudes or motivate them to upgrade their knowledge, which turns them into culturally illiterate persons carrying worthless university degrees.

> In contrast, education that comes with the right attitudes, such as respecting work and time, appreciating material gain, protecting the environment, and caring for the poor, is likely to increase labor productivity. Young men and women armed with the right education and attitudes are not only assets capable of making progress but also valuable social tools to teach illiterate parents many things and help less educated friends and neighbors to understand and appreciate new facts of life. By so doing, they lead society to become more economically productive and socially, politically, and environmentally aware.[4]

The human brain is the most valuable asset that every person has; and treating it as such is the right way to ensure mental development, career advancement, personal satisfaction, and a rich life. People who ignore their brains and shy away from acquiring more knowledge and gaining more experience are wasting the most valuable assets they have; an asset upon which they rely to succeed in life. In the wake of the 2004 Tsunami that hit several Asian countries including Indonesia, a former Indonesian student of mine sent me an email reminding me of a statement I had made in the class he attended, and to tell me that that statement was instrumental in helping him face many challenges. The statement says, "We teach you here not to make you change your minds, but to train you how to use your brains." The Tsunami in question "was the deadliest in recorded history, taking 230,000 lives in a matter of hours."[5]

Smart people do not sit back and let things happen to them; they do not wait for opportunities to come knocking at their doors. Instead, they get involved, take the initiative, and make things happen for them; they are always focused on their careers and future, always able to recognize opportunities and create new ones to exploit. They do every task with eagerness and enthusiasm as if they are doing it for the very first time, always striving for perfection. If we were to use this behavior to evaluate the attitudes of university graduates in the Third World, we are most likely to discover that only a tiny percentage leave university with the right knowledge and attitude to strive for perfection.

Traditional societies are generally more conservative and religious and therefore, they tend to emphasize education that reinforces traditions and traditional values; they also tend to give religious and historical subjects priority over most other branches of knowledge. People who are still living in preindustrial times usually rely on traditional wisdom and old knowledge, which is a function of very old cultural values, customs, and life experiences, not of scientific knowledge. Being a product of memories and certain life experiences of a long-gone past, traditional wisdom has become, especially after the dawn of the Internet and the mapping of human genes and the technology of smart phones, irrelevant, even to people who are still living in its times. Because of that, traditional wisdom has become an obstacle to economic development, sociocultural transformation, and rational thinking. Unlike scientific knowledge, which is a liberating force, traditional wisdom is a force of social repression and political oppression.

Resources that a nation may have are useful only if people know how to evaluate them, how to use them, and how to employ them where they are most needed, or where the benefits are most rewarding. Though people can and often learn and borrow from each other, their training of how to learn, how to apply what is learned, and what kind of knowledge matters most, is most important to determining the usefulness of the knowledge they acquire and value of the resources they may have. These are questions of culture and its value and belief systems, which by defining priorities, determine what is to be learned, how much to be learned, and how much freedom the learned should have in applying the knowledge they learn.

Social Transformation in the Knowledge Age

At the time of writing this book in January 2023, the living conditions in many countries of the world have reached a dynamic state of change; technologies to enhance our abilities to deal with every aspect of life are being developed at the speed of light. Countless individuals, social forces, institutions, and organizations, having varied, oftentimes contradictory interests, are leading this development process. As a consequence, a "world in transition" has emerged, where impersonal, non-institutional, and non-ideological forces have assumed a leading role in instigating change, causing conflict, and producing social transformations of great proportions and implications. This has caused ideologies and deep convictions and belief systems to lose much of their power to initiate change and cause profound transformations in life. Whatever change such ideologies and convictions may produce is more likely to deepen conflict and lead people to incorrectly believe that history is capable of reversing itself, and that a future could be constructed on a vision of a glorious, yet fading and largely fictitious, past.

Today's knowledge society is characterized by complexity, diversity, and dynamism. Complexity causes systems to fail and forces them to restructure continuously; diversity deepens sociocultural divides and socioeconomic gaps in society and creates and recreates new antagonisms and sociocultural groups continuously. Dynamism, meanwhile, makes both change and conflict around the world an uncontrollable process that affects human values, interests, and relationships at all levels, at all times. No ideology, no leader, no system, no plan, and no state, therefore, can manage change by itself; and history no longer has the tools or knowledge to explain the present or predict the future.

As the age of knowledge advances, it expands the horizons and multiplies the opportunities open to us on the one hand and challenges our basic and most revered values and traditions on the other. In about 3 years from now, I believe that the knowledge age will reach maturity and everyone in the world will have felt its impact. Satellite communications are increasingly becoming cheaper and more available everywhere, and sophisticated knowledge is becoming accessible to anyone who can afford it and knows how to use it. For example, the mapping of the human genes, which was completed in 2000, will enable us to fight many diseases and manipulate our own genes as well as the genes of plants and animals, and thus enhance our ability to influence the physical characteristics and levels of intelligence of humans and animals alike. Self-driven cars will make cities cleaner, while causing millions of taxi and truck drivers to lose their jobs. A new, very complex society and a new, highly diversified culture are emerging fast and changing our way of life and perceptions of it drastically and irreversibly.

Socioeconomic development, to be feasible, needs more than traditional education, or the abundance of natural resources, or the availability of cheap labor, or a fairly developed infrastructure, or even a good supply of capital. It needs a society whose values are conducive to change, whose human resources are skilled and disciplined, and whose institutions are capable of designing and carrying out reform plans and leading change. No nation has so far managed to industrialize without experiencing profound social and cultural transformations, and no socially and culturally developed nation has failed to enter the industrial age.

Michael Young describes in a book published in 1951 '*The rise of the Meritocracy*,' "a future dystopian society in which intelligence and merit would become the central tenet of society, replacing previous divisions of social class and creating a society stratified between a merited power-holding elite and a disenfranchised underclass of the less merited. The elite status is becoming hereditary. Now, there is no longer any hope because a person's ability is known even before he or she is born. The conservatives want this hereditary status to continue."[6]

Michael Young says further that "equality of opportunity, which was promoted as an alternative to the utopian concept of total equality in society, can neither help the poor nor can it protect the needy. Equal opportunity serves to divide society into two groups: One is capable of seizing the opportunity offered to it; the other is incapable of seizing its opportunity. Because of this inability, the second group finds itself moving downward and forming a largely poor and neglected class. But unlike any other class in human history, the new class is neither enslaved, nor exploited, not even officially excluded. It is rather free yet excluded, has opportunities yet poor, lives in an open society, yet cannot move upward on the social ladder. It is, as a result, permanently left behind, deprived even of a cause to rally around."[7]

The emergence and plight of this class is not the result of certain actions taken by any state; therefore, state action alone cannot change the living conditions and fortunes of the poor. Fundamental structural changes in the social order are needed to make it possible for this class of people to move upward and be included. American capitalism and democracy, for example, have created two separate islands within America; one is characterized by affluence and security; the other is characterized by poverty and violence. While both islands live side by side in most cities, they are socially and culturally separated by several decades if not centuries.

The association of wealth with knowledge in today's modern society is probably the single most important factor contributing to creating this class and keeping it permanently behind. People with knowledge, that is, people with the right education and attitudes are able to seize opportunities, make more money, gain more power, and move upward. In addition, people with money, that is people with the economic means, have the resources to get the best education and knowledge available and expand the range of opportunities open to them. In contrast, people with neither wealth nor knowledge are left behind, with nothing to enable them to compete and move upward in society. The future, therefore, is not expected to see nations divided between rich and poor. Instead, it is more likely to see people divided between knowledgeable and ignorant; the first is rich and free, the second is poor and anything but free.

The widening sociocultural divides and the deepening socioeconomic gaps in society are causing intellectuals and the masses to feel alienated from each other. The life experiences of the two groups are growing increasingly divergent due to their different knowledge, traditions, values, languages, and outlooks. As a result, communication between the masses and intellectuals is growing more difficult every day, causing miscommunication and mutual mistrust to spread and deepen. While the masses tend to doubt the honesty of intellectuals in general, intellectuals tend to doubt the rationality of the masses in particular. This leaves the masses without a leadership they can understand and trust; and deprives intellectuals of their most important cause.

The poor, consequently, are increasingly being seen as a liability and largely responsible for their misery and because the poor can be isolated and are in fact being isolated, and since the rich can be insulated and are in fact being insulated, the poor have become largely invisible; they are being ignored and forgotten, getting neither the attention they deserve nor the compassion they need. New attitudes and cultural values, and unconventional societal systems are needed to deal with the problems of the poor and the excluded people in society. Education that emphasizes work ethics and discipline and provides students with the right knowledge and attitudes is a powerful tool to change the social and economic structures in society, help alleviate the suffering of the poor, enhance the security of the rich, and improve the quality of life for all.

People engaged in the development of knowledge are faced with a difficult challenge. They need to make themselves understood by those who have little knowledge and make knowledge and the technologies they develop accessible to those with little money to buy it. There is need also to make knowledge capable of addressing the particular needs of people who need it most but can afford it and use it least. While institutions are the tools to produce knowledge, the right education is the means to deliver knowledge to people and make it relevant. On the other hand, the right attitudes are qualities that make people with knowledge able to help themselves and others and improve the quality of life for all humans.

Reforming the Education System

No society can develop and achieve satisfactory levels of economic, social, cultural, scientific, and political transformation without the right education. Generally speaking, there is no society with a low literacy rate that is developed and no society with a high literacy rate that is underdeveloped. However, there are many societies in the Middle East and Latin America with relatively high rates of literacy that have failed to develop and industrialize because their education systems are underdeveloped, and their cultures are traditional. Several Arab states have fairly high literacy rates, yet they are still struggling to complete the transition from the agricultural to the industrial age. These states suffer from two major disadvantages: education systems that transform most human resources from untapped assets into liabilities, and sociocultural environments that create and perpetuate cultural illiteracy.

To make societal development possible, education should be made compulsory for both boys and girls through at least the ninth grade, and money should be made available to build comfortable schools, adopt modern methods of instruction, upgrade the contents of curricula, and make school coeducational. The education system needs to recognize that the majority of students do not know how to organize their thoughts and manage their time. Schools and universities, therefore, must design special academic programs and nonacademic activities to address these issues. The education system must also recognize that teaching research methodology and scientific curiosity starts in the first grade, not in university or in high school. Changing attitudes through education and nonacademic activities is possible if education teaches students how to use their brains, get used to teamwork, and learn how to find information they need when they need it, while inducing them to think critically and be creative. Education that uses classrooms to reinforce traditional ways of thinking and glorify the past makes social transformation more difficult.

Cultural Illiteracy

Illiteracy is traditionally defined as the inability to read and write. But illiteracy should be divided into types: Traditional illiteracy and cultural illiteracy, both of which need serious attention. "Cultural illiteracy" is defined as a lack of general awareness of life conditions related to health, work, education, politics, economics, knowledge, scientific facts, literature, the arts, and most global developments. For example, Arab students seldom read books, they usually read required textbooks to pass examinations at the end of the year, and only a tiny minority shows interest in acquiring reading as a habit and a source of pleasure. Therefore, students need to be taught how to read and enjoy reading because acquiring the habit of reading serves three objectives: it helps transform students' attitudes faster; it addresses the problem of cultural illiteracy early; and it invigorates book writing and publishing, which is a financially and socially rewarding activity that creates new jobs. If reading were to become a hobby practiced by students and the public, book publishing would grow quickly and create a large number of good jobs annually and, in the process, vastly reduce cultural illiteracy and remove an obstacle that transforms human resources from potential assets to actual liabilities.

A program to end cultural illiteracy in a country like Egypt over a twenty-year period would cause book publishing in Egypt to increase by at least five times in the first year alone and create about 160,000 jobs, assuming that every 1500 copies of each book create one new job. Thereafter, the book publishing industry would grow by about 15% annually, creating about four million jobs over ten years. About 3 million of those jobs would come from book writing, editing, translating, printing, publishing and binding, and sales and marketing. Another 1 million jobs would be created by associated business services, such as finance and accounting, public relations, computer programming, export–import of books and educational materials, and paper manufacturing. What is unique about this industry and the jobs it creates is that it can be developed without state investment or involvement. All that is needed is issuing a law that makes reading books a required subject like math and languages. Egypt's population exceeded 102 million in 2020, with an illiteracy rate of 14.4% for males and 26% for females.

States with high rates of illiteracy and concerned international organizations recognize traditional illiteracy and acknowledge its drawbacks; however, cultural illiteracy is still far from being understood by states and international organizations; in fact, I coined the term "cultural illiteracy" 15 years ago and explained its nature and implications in a book published in 2010. Since this concept is new, awareness of the existence of cultural illiteracy and its negative effects on society is still missing. I believe that more than 90% of all high school and university graduates in the Third World are culturally illiterate. This problem was created two generations ago due primarily to the spread of poverty, lack of schools, and dependence on traditional leaders to manage community and national affairs.

Though the building of millions of schools and thousands of universities worldwide has reduced traditional illiteracy, it failed to recognize the cultural illiteracy problem and solve it. In fact, traditional systems of education have perpetuated cultural illiteracy and spread its negative impact. Education that emphasizes memorization of largely boring information on the one hand, and families entertained and educated by TV programs that dull the minds on the other have caused cultural illiteracy to deepen its roots in society and become structural in most developing countries. Lack of incentives to read books during the school and college years caused cultural illiteracy to replace traditional illiteracy as a major force causing backwardness; it also leads most graduates to lose within years most of what they learned in their schools and colleges.

In traditional societies, people who are illiterate tend to show modesty and accept modest jobs because they know their limitations. In contrast, college graduates plagued with cultural illiteracy tend to feel that society owes them a great debt, and, consequently, they expect positions with power, which they often use to denigrate and sometimes humiliate the less educated and the poor. Cultural illiteracy leads naturally to scientific, technological, health, and financial illiteracy. As the global economy shifts from manufacturing goods to producing knowledge and information, the most rewarding jobs it creates require learning special skills and advanced knowledge. People who are scientifically and technologically illiterate cannot find and hold good jobs, which causes them to feel frustrated and angry. In addition, culturally illiterate people are less able to live productive lives, get enough self-satisfaction, and relate to the larger world in meaningful and intelligent ways. To begin to solve the cultural illiteracy problem, reading must be made compulsory; no student should be allowed to graduate from high school without completing it.

The following is a visionary plan to accomplish four major objectives: First, help students change their attitudes and acquire reading as a habit while exposing them to scientific facts and new ideas and ways of thinking. Second, move education beyond the memorization stage and into the critical thinking stage. Third, facilitate attitudinal change while reducing cultural illiteracy among the public at large. Fourth, create millions of new jobs year after year and better citizens. According to the proposed plan, schools, universities, educators, intellectuals, and the media would work together to make the necessary arrangements while the state makes the implementation of such arrangements by schools and universities compulsory. The following describes the proposed arrangements:

1. Students in grades 3–6 would be required to read two books during summer vacations and write a report on each book to be presented to their teacher at the beginning of the next school year. Students would be given a list of five books to choose from; books would be selected by a national panel of educators and intellectuals to cover five different fields, such as history, geography, nature, and literature.
2. Students in grades 7–9 would be required to read three books each summer and write a report on each one, summarizing the major points and the lessons they learned; the report would be presented to the school administrator at the beginning of the next school year. Students would be given seven books to choose from; a different panel of educators and intellectuals would choose books that cover seven fields of study, such as sociology, economics, space, and culture.
3. Students in grades 10–12 would be required to read four books each summer and write a report on each one, critically analyzing the major points of each book; the report would be presented to the school administrator at the beginning of the next school year. Students would be given ten books to choose from; a different panel of educators, intellectuals, scientists, and businesspeople would choose these books. Some of the books must challenge the intellectual capacities of students and cover topics such as comparative religion, philosophy, and science fiction. In addition, each student would be required to complete twenty hours of community service each year, helping the poor, the elderly, the sick, or working for not-for-profit organizations protecting the environment or caring for animals. All students would be required to write a report about their experience in community service and make a class presentation of their findings during the last semester before graduation.
4. Students in college would be required to read two books each semester dealing with topics not related to their majors and present their findings during the last week of the school year in special classes. In addition, college students would be required to complete at least twenty hours of community service each semester and two weeks in each summer. They would also be required to complete a

research project on a topic related to their field of study and present their findings in a report to be shared with and discussed by fellow students before graduation.

As for the university, the following would be required:

- Design on-campus projects to train students to engage in business and develop their work ethics and entrepreneurial spirits and skills. University should make most services like library assistants, restaurant, security, cleaning, maintenance, transportation, and gardening business projects available to students to work for, manage, and profit from. No student, however, should be allowed to continue working for such projects after graduation.
- Give a financial reward to the best managed project each year and special recognition to all students involved in it.
- Require that professors assign at least three textbooks or two books and 4–6 articles for each course in the humanities, social sciences, and business.
- Ban smoking and alcohol drinking for all students and faculty members and staff in all buildings, at all times; and
- Participate in establishing, financing, and managing a new foundation, to be called Foundation for Publishing, Research, and Translation (FPRT). Universities would be required to contribute to financing FPRT by paying the equivalent of one hundred dollars per student per year. As for the state, it is required to conduct an annual competition for reading for all school students and grant winners financial rewards in addition to taking them on educational trips to other countries. The business community should be urged to sponsor the competition and the trips. The state is also required to enact a new law requiring all public corporations to pay 1% of their annual net profits to FPRT. FPRT would be managed by a board of trustees composed of retired professors, university presidents, and businesspeople chosen on the basis of competence, integrity, and commitment to scientific research. Faculty members and researchers from inside and outside all universities would have equal opportunities to compete for grants. The business community would be encouraged to become a partner in managing FPRT and proposing research topics. FPRT is required to publish not less than 5000 new

titles each year, about a third of which are translations from foreign languages.

Since almost all schools in the Third World lack professional management, a new college to train school administrators should be established. The college, to be called School Management College or SMC, would be commissioned by the state to do three major things: develop a school management system, train qualified teachers to manage schools and teach specific topics, and continually upgrade teaching methods and curricula. The proposed college would grant an executive master of school management (MSM) degree in preschool, elementary and middle school, and high school administration. SMC would accept only highly competent teachers who are college graduates and have completed at least five years of teaching experience. Egypt has over 60,000 schools, but very few of them are managed by competent administrators. If the principal and his or her deputy were required to be MSM holders, replacing all current principals and deputies with professionally trained ones over ten years would require training about 15,000 administrators a year.

SMC would establish campuses in major cities and have three different programs: an evening program to attract teachers with families, a weekend program to attract teachers who need to travel but are able to devote their weekends to learning, and a summer program to attract young teachers willing to commit most of their summer vacations to learning. Each program would have practical and theoretical parts that include teaching administrators how to evaluate the performance of other teachers and school personnel, how to manage libraries, and how to work with teachers and staff to design nonacademic activities to help students discover their talents and manage their time while enjoying their school experiences.

Healthcare

According to countless reports issued by many international organizations like the International Finance Corporation (IFC), the World Bank, and the World Health Organization, and other private and public agencies, healthcare in most parts of the world is in a very bad shape, and consequently people, particularly the poor and the old are suffering. But if we consider the financial and human and technological resources and the experience we have, it becomes clear that we should not have such a problem. There is no doubt that most problems that we are facing today are difficult, but there is no healthcare problem that cannot be solved; what prevents us from solving this problem is lack of political will, and cultures that do not view the other as deserving equal rights, and greed that drives the rich and large corporations to worship money and close their eyes whenever they see a poor person begging or a sick child crying or a mother sweeping streets while carrying her child on her back.

IFC says; "Health care in Sub-Saharan Africa remains the worst in the world, with few countries able to spend the $34 to $40 a year per person that the World Health Organization considers the minimum for basic health care. And despite widespread poverty, an astonishing 50% of the region's health expenditure is financed by out-of-pocket payments from individuals."[8] The report finds that the private sector already delivers about half of Africa's health products and services, which means that the state is abandoning the people and failing to honor its commitment to its citizens.

According to the Economist Intelligence Unit, African countries "face very complex healthcare challenges as they seek to manage a range of infectious diseases, while at the same time grappling with the growth of non-communicable diseases and accidents, all against a backdrop of health systems that are substantially underdeveloped compared with those in other regions. In the Middle East, meanwhile, there is a contrast between the wealthy Gulf States, in which chronic disease is the central health challenge, and other parts of the region, where less developed health systems and strained resources challenge policymakers. Meanwhile, continued low levels of public financing for health mean that public-sector facilities are often overburdened, and the quality of care remains low in many places."[9]

Another study done by the University of Washington says that Arab countries "have made some significant health gains over the past two decades, including increases in life expectancy and swift reductions in child mortality. But the rise of chronic diseases, diet-related risk factors, and deaths from road injuries threatens that progress. Health reforms with a focus on prevention are urgently needed; smoking stands out for its toll on health. As motor vehicle use grows in the Arab world, road injuries are an increasing cause of disease burden. In high-income countries, road injuries were not only a leading cause of death but also a leading cause of premature mortality and disability. Dietary risks were the leading risk factors for death in all of the region's high-income countries with the exception of Saudi Arabia, where elevated blood pressure ranked higher. The Arab countries are in transition from places where infectious diseases are the main cause of concern to places where heart disease, cancer, and diabetes are the main worries."[10]

According to reports issued by the World Bank, life expectancy has risen in every country during the last three decades. However, healthcare did not improve as fast to keep most people healthy, particularly during old age. In the meantime, growing awareness of the importance of healthcare to the quality of life and the productivity of labor on the one hand, and the lack of adequate healthcare in most countries of the world on the other has created a healthcare crisis in the poor countries. However, traditional cultures in such countries were able to take care of older and sick people and therefore protect the dignity of man. But these traditional cultures are changing fast due to pressure caused by several forces: the adoption of the free market philosophy, the widening gap between the rich and poor, and the promotion of the culture of consumption at the expense of the culture of production. The pressure applied by these forces is causing deep sociocultural, sociopolitical, and socioeconomic transformations in every society and this has caused greed and lust for money and power to spread and be accepted, while causing ethics and the sense of community and social responsibility to decline. As a consequence, the way people live, think, and view the world and the other today has changed fundamentally. This calls for new and more efficient healthcare delivery systems, more physicians and qualified healthcare workers, and above all, the recognition of healthcare as a basic human right.

Globally, the World Health Organization (WHO) "estimates a shortage of 4.3 million physicians, nurses and other health workers worldwide, especially in developing countries. Developing nations often have physician shortages due to limited numbers and capacity of medical schools and because of international migration: physicians can usually earn much more money and enjoy better working conditions in other countries. Many developed countries also report doctor shortages, and this traditionally happens in rural and underserved areas. In the US alone, the Association of American Medical Colleges (AAMC) estimates a shortage of 91,500 physicians by 2020."[11]

In the meantime, the ratio of physicians to patients ranges from hundreds to many thousands. For example, while the ratio is 1 physician to 210 persons in Cuba; the ratio in Tanzania is 1 physician to 50,000 persons. In the highest tiers come Greece at 1 to 227; Russia at 1 to 235, Italy at 1 to 238; Germany at 1 to 290; the United States at 1 to 500; and China at 1 to 600. In the lowest tiers come Tanzania at 1 to 50,000;

Ethiopia at 1 to 33,000; Chad at 1 to 25,000; and in the middle tiers come Thailand at 1 to 2700; Morocco at 1 to 2000; Egypt at 1 to 1900; and India at 1 to 1700.[12]

The above health indicators clearly suggest that the healthcare situation for the majority of the world population is not good; in fact, healthcare is deteriorating in countries that are witnessing war and conflict, and others that have high rates of population growth. The main things that people of such countries need most are health awareness and disease prevention. In addition, there is a need to share experiences among the states of each region with similar cultures, geography, weather conditions, and diet. Above all, they need outside help from the states that recognize healthcare as a universal human right and are able to develop and manage efficient healthcare delivery systems, like Western European states; such states should help needy countries to restructure their healthcare systems and train enough physicians and healthcare workers to manage them.

States should provide universal health care and free education to all citizens. Many people would argue that no state can afford paying for the education and healthcare of every citizen; this claim is false and often dishonest. The argument against free education and healthcare is an ideological argument; not an economic or social one. In fact, no state pays for the services it provides its citizens; the state levies taxes from citizens and uses the revenues to pay for the services it provides. This means that states collect taxes on behalf of people, divide revenues among the many programs, and manage how money is spent. People who oppose universal healthcare and free education are usually the rich who oppose levying enough taxes to cover state expenses. Those people do not believe in equal opportunity; and do not care about anything except making more money, accumulating wealth, and using the wealth and the power it generates to influence the law and change it in their favor.

The latest report issued by Oxfam on January 17, 2023 says: "As the world's corporate and political elite convened in Davos, Switzerland for the first winter World Economic Forum in three years, an analysis published Monday by Oxfam International found that the global rich have captured nearly two-thirds of all wealth generated since 2020—a period marked by a devastating pandemic, worsening costs of living crises, and continued fallout from the climate emergency. Oxfam shows that the top 1% worldwide grabbed $26 trillion of the $42 trillion in new wealth created, close to twice as much as the bottom 99% of the global population. Billionaires, in particular, have seen their wealth explode since 2020, adding around $1.7 million to their net worth for every $1 in wealth gained by a person in the bottom 90% of the global income distribution. According to Oxfam, billionaires' fortunes have grown by an average of $2.7 billion per day since 2020."[13]

In contrast, people who support free education and universal healthcare believe in equal opportunity and see it as a necessary condition for having educated, healthy, and loyal citizens. In fact, without a healthy and well-educated population, particularly in this age, every economy will be less innovative and competitive; and most people will be less active and productive. Citizens who cannot afford healthcare or decent education are unable to live comfortable lives because they have to worry about what might happen to them when they get sick and old, how to get a decent job without adequate skills; and how to help their children get good education and climb the social ladder.

There are many states in the world, like Germany and the Scandinavian states that provide universal healthcare and free education to their people. Though every state can afford universal healthcare and free education, systems of delivering these services are not the same everywhere; in fact, they need not be the same. To provide comprehensive healthcare and free education, states need to enact tax laws capable of generating enough revenues to pay for public programs. Failure to provide universal healthcare and free education will cause the socioeconomic gaps in society to widen, and the sociocultural divides to deepen; and that would undermine the democratic system, encourage radicalism, and cause social conflict that, when prolonged, often leads to unrest and violence; France under Macron is a good example of such an eventuality.

Any serious attempt to reform the healthcare delivery system in any state must start by asking two basic questions:

First, what services do health insurance companies provide to the public, or what do such companies do to serve their members and doctors. Anyone who deals with health insurance companies knows that the only thing they do is to intervene at every level of service, telling patients what is covered and what is not, and telling doctors what they should and should not do. Since neither patients nor doctors like to be told what to do, or see companies question their feelings and integrity, both patients and doctors often go around the system to get what they feel they are entitled to. As a result, fraud, waste, inefficiency, and high premiums have become an aspect of healthcare systems that rely on insurance companies. Health insurance companies are middlemen who make the experience of patients and doctors costly and unpleasant in order to make unearned money. Since such companies provide no useful service whatsoever, no one needs them, and everyone will do much better without them. Therefore, health Insurance companies have no business being in the healthcare business.

Second, is healthcare a basic human right that all members of society are entitled to? I certainly believe so. However, for a credible evaluation of this issue, we need to look at it from two angles: the human rights perspective and the economic perspective.

If a poor person has a serious, yet curable health problem that threatens his life, and society refuses to provide him with the required medical help, he is more likely to die in pain. Failure to provide such a person with the healthcare he needs means that society causes some of its members to suffer needlessly and die prematurely. Such an act amounts to a collective decision by society to discriminate against the sick and poor, even if that means wasting a human life and its potential contribution to society. From a purely economic viewpoint, investing money to educate someone who suffers from an incurable disease amounts to wasting money needlessly. In fact, a person with such a health condition, while costing more money to educate, is unlikely to perform well in school or use whatever skills he may acquire to contribute to society. But since education is acknowledged as a basic human right by all nations, society is obligated to provide such a person with an equal opportunity to education. The question then boils down to this: why should society pay to educate a person, knowing in advance that that person would not be able to make a meaningful contribution to society, and not help another person who has the potential to contribute to the welfare of society if given the medical assistance he needs to cure an ailment and save his life?

When an educated but poor person gets very sick and society refuses to provide him with the medical care he needs, society often loses all the money it has invested in educating that person, as well as his potential contribution to society. This simply means that keeping people healthy is a prerequisite to keeping them productive; and helping people to become creative and productive necessitates providing them with the right education and adequate healthcare. While an educated person cannot contribute to the welfare of society unless he is healthy to think and work, a healthy person can contribute to the welfare of society even if he is illiterate; healthcare therefore comes before education. Any society that refuses to help its suffering members and let them live in pain and die in despair is a harsh society that does not value human life and does not belong to the civilized world.

Notes

1. https://www.commonwealthfund.org/publications/issue-briefs/2017/oct/how-well-does-insurance-coverage-protect-consumers-health-care.
2. Mohamed Rabie, *A Theory of Sustainable Sociocultural and Economic Development*, Palgrave Macmillan, 2016, 145.
3. David Landes, "Culture Makes Almost All the Difference," in *Culture Matters: How Values Shape Human Progress*, eds. Lawrence E. Harrison and Samuel Huntington, Basic Books, 2000, 13.
4. Mohamed Rabie, *A Theory of Sustainable Sociocultural and Economic Development*, Palgrave Macmillan, 2016, 148.
5. https://www.history.com/news/deadliest-tsunami-2004-indian-ocean.
6. Young, Michael (28 June 2001). "Down with meritocracy". *The Guardian*.
7. Mohamed Rabie; Education and Social Transformation; www.yazour.com) 15.
8. Health Care in Africa: IFC Report. Sees Demand for Investment. https://www.ifc.org/wps/wcm/connect/news_ext_content/ifc_external_corporate_site/news+and+events/healthafricafeature.
9. http://accesstohealthcare.eiu.com/wpcontent/uploads/sites/42/2017/06/AccesstohealthcareinAfricaandtheMiddleEast.pdf.
10. Ali Mokdad Arab countries living longer but battling chronic disease. http://www.healthdata.org/news-release/arab-countries-living-longer-battling-chronic-disease.
11. Physician Supply, Wikipedia. https://en.wikipedia.org/wiki/Physician_supply.
12. NationMaster; Health > physician > per 1000 people: country compared. https://www.nationmaster.com/country-info/stats/Health/Physicians/Per-1%2C000-people).
13. Jake Johnson, Billionaires have seen their wealth skyrocket over the past two years, adding roughly $2.7 billion per day to their fortunes while ordinary people struggle to afford basic necessities. January 17, 2023. https://www.commondreams.org/news/billionaires-policy-failure-oxfam.

CHAPTER 13

Developing the Sustainability Concept

Abstract This chapter, recognizing the importance of sustainable development to our world and humanity, tries to clarify and emphasize issues related to sustainable development. It reviews the available literature on sustainability, and gives the reader sufficient information on how states, international organizations, including the United Nations, and corporations view it and try to deal with it. So this chapter is more informative than innovative; it explains and clarifies complicated issues, identifies the major parties that take sustainability seriously, tells the history of the sustainability concept, and helps everyone understand where most states, political leaders, corporations, civil society organizations, and social scientists stand. Authors of the first report on sustainability said, "we are searching for a model output that represents a world system that is: 1. sustainable without sudden and uncontrolled collapse; and 2. capable of satisfying the basic material requirements of all of its people." However, the agreed upon types of Sustainability are Social Sustainability, Economic Sustainability, Environmental Sustainability, and Cultural Sustainability.

Keywords Sustainability · Club of Rome · Limits to Growth · Consumption rates · Reducing Waste · Brundtland Commission · Legrand Group · UNESCO · Biodiversity · Cultural Diversity · US Environmental Protection Agency

M. Rabie, *A Future Economy for All*,
https://doi.org/10.1007/978-3-031-42957-6_13

Literature on sustainable development reveals that economic sustainability was the point of departure for sustainability studies in general; this led people concerned to realize that no economic development could be sustainable without taking the state of the environment into consideration. Since all actions to deal with both spheres of sustainability are taken by people to serve their interests and the interests of others, social sustainability became an integral component of sustainability; and since people actions are influenced by their cultural backgrounds, cultural sustainability was later recognized as a component of sustainable development. Consequently, the four types of sustainability must be viewed as four facets of one issue that concerns peoples everywhere, which dictates coordination of actions and integration of public and private policies. Therefore, building a sustainable world should be viewed as a project to use the human, natural, cultural, and social capital available to us to ensure a balanced, stable, and peaceful world. But while no one and no state controls these resources, economic interdependence, and global connections dictate that sustainability should be sought at the global level.

In 1972, the Club of Rome issued a report on the state of the world using the "sustainable" concept for the first time. "*The Limits to Growth*" report was authored by a group of scientists led by Dennis and Donnella Meadows in which they described the desirable "state of global equilibrium." Since then the report was updated more than once in which the same issues were highlighted, and a strong argument was made not to "overshoot" while doing anything. Yes, the world condition did not deteriorate as fast as predicted in 1972; but climate change, resource grab, war, and some of the new technologies have made our world less human, less peaceful, less equitable, and thus less sustainable economically, environmentally, socially, and culturally.

Authors of the first report wrote, "We are searching for a model output that represents a world system that is: (1) sustainable without sudden and uncontrolled collapse; and (2) capable of satisfying the basic material requirements of all of its people."[1] This definition views sustainability as an economic issue only. But developing a world system where a state of equilibrium prevails requires balancing economic production, peoples' actions and desires, and nature's ability to renew depleted resources, when no one can determine the feasible rate of resource extraction or the actual rate of resource renewal or control people's actions or even knows their desires.

"*The Limits to Growth*" sought to highlight the dangers inherent in high economic growth and consumption rates that cause natural resources to be depleted at a rate that exceeds nature's ability to replenish. Though this argument makes sense, some people denied the claim that resources are being depleted faster than nature's ability to replenish them; others argued that market regulations at the time prevented the optimum allocation of resources, which lead to adopting the disastrous free market economy in the 1980s; and many more called for stricter environmental regulations and reducing waste.

In 1987, the *Brundtland Commission* issued a report on the state of the world's environment and development, in which it used the term "sustainable development" for the first time. The commission defined sustainable development as "development that meets the needs of the present without compromising the ability of future generations to meet their own needs."[2] Michael Needham goes beyond this definition to say that sustainable development is "the ability to meet the needs of the present while contributing to [meeting] the future generations' needs."[3] Therefore, sustainable development could be defined as "a pattern of economic growth in which resource use aims to meet the present human needs while preserving the environment so it can meet the needs of future generations."

Since issues of public concern are inherently controversial, the issue of "sustainable development" continues to be debated. Forces promoting environmental protection and defend the rights of the poor, and others promoting free markets have caused three conflicting worldviews to emerge. The first worldview emphasizes environmental protection and calls for regulations to protect nature from degradation; the second emphasizes free markets and claims that the sustainability notion is too vague to be helpful and that markets are by their nature optimizers. The third worldview says that constructing a world system in equilibrium with nature requires that the developed nations start contracting their economies to allow the developing ones to expand their economies while preserving the environment and enabling the world system to meet the basic needs of all peoples and avoid sudden collapse.

In 2005, the UN held a summit to study issues of development; the declaration issued by the summit refers to three interdependent and mutually reinforcing pillars of sustainable development; they are economic development, social development, and environmental protection.[4] The Legrand Group says that "In the field of sustainable development, there are many major challenges to be addressed. They require us to re-think our economy and our growth in favor of a society that is more economical in its use of raw materials and energy. Some of these challenges include climate change, energy consumption, waste production, threats to public health, poverty, social exclusion, management of natural resources, loss of biodiversity, and land use."[5]

Robert Takes and others argue that "opponents of sustainable development attack from two different perspectives. While some view sustainable development as a top-down attempt by the United Nations to dictate how the people of the world should live their lives—and thus as a threat to individual freedoms and property rights: others view it as capitulation that implies development as usual, driven by the interests of big business that pays only lip service to social justice and the protection of nature."[6] In a study; "*Our Common Journey: A Transition toward Sustainability*," the Board on Sustainable Development of the US National Academy of Sciences identified three major categories it claims need to be developed to realize sustainability; they are nature, life support systems, and community; in other words, economy, the environment, and people.

Though debate over issues of sustainable development led to defining the sustainability problem as how to manage three types of capital; economic, social, and natural; the indigenous peoples of the world argued that sustainable development has four pillars, the fourth being cultural. *The Universal Declaration on Cultural Diversity*, issued by UNESCO in 2001, states, "Cultural diversity is as necessary for humankind as biodiversity is for nature. In this sense, it is the common heritage of humanity and should be recognized and affirmed for the benefit of present and future generations... [it is] one of the roots of development understood not simply in terms of economic growth, but also as a means to achieve a more satisfactory intellectual, emotional, moral and spiritual existence"[7] But as production and consumption activities deplete our shared natural capital like water and minerals, globalization undermines our cultural capital as it pollutes and deforms indigenous cultures.

I believe that the definition of the 2005 UN summit on development has clarified the issues of sustainability and made it easier for us to view and deal with them constructively. By identifying economic development, social development, and environmental protection as interdependent and mutually reinforcing pillars of sustainable development, the report gave us a clear path to follow. While the Club or Rome report emphasized the economic dimension of sustainability, the Brundtland Commission report added an environmental dimension to the economic one; the UN summit added social sustainability as a third dimension, and the indigenous people added culture as a fourth dimension. Despite the importance of each dimension, I believe that the social dimension is the most important and relevant one.

Economic Sustainability

It is true that the Brundtland Commission provided a clear definition of sustainable development, but it could not answer questions related to how to achieve sustainability, nor could the experts who tried later to elaborate on it. No one in fact can say with confidence how to reach a state of sustainability or what are the needs of future generations that we must consider. No one also knows how many people will be there at any time in the future; how much resources will be available at that time; or what the state of technology will be years from today. We also do not know how much progress we are making at this point, or when a state of sustainability is expected to be reached. Indeed, we do not even know if we are moving closer to sustainable development or moving away from it. But despite the complicated nature of these questions, we cannot ignore them. Therefore, I shall try to answer some of these questions, and explain why sustainable development must be considered a global issue.

The Legrand Group report says that "The concept of sustainable development is based on a set of requirements. It must allow the basic needs of present and future generations to be fulfilled, such as access to water, education, health, employment, and the fight against hunger." The report argues further that development should aim to improve the quality of life, which involves easier access to medical care and social services and "respect for rights and freedoms and the promotion of new forms of renewable energy such as wind, solar, and geothermal power."[8] The report goes on to say that "sustainable development involves narrowing the gaps between rich and poor countries, because these gaps, if maintained or accentuated, could cause violent conflicts, which by their very nature lead to regression rather than development."[9] It is clear that the Legrand Group views sustainability as a comprehensive global process that covers the economic and social and environmental aspects of life. Nevertheless, this report, just like other reports, fails to provide a plan of action to reach sustainability.

The first attempt to reach common understandings regarding issues of sustainability began as negotiations between the rich and poor nations, with each group suspecting the intentions of the other. While the poor nations viewed the rich nations' repeated calls for the protection of the environment as an attempt to deny them the opportunity to grow their economies and develop their societies; the rich nations viewed the poor nations' determination to grow their economies as a threat to the environment and its scarce natural resources. Nevertheless, nations agreed on a joint view at the Rio conference of 1992. But since what is feasible today is unlikely to be feasible tomorrow, "sustainability should be viewed and treated as a special global state in transition that describes a wishful state of nature and a desired way of living and coexisting in harmony."[10] Societal and global developments are evolving processes that transform all aspects of life, and involve all actors whose actions affect life, such as people, technology, culture, and weather; they also involve actors affected by nature and human actions, such as water resources, the environment, and the air we breathe.

Despite all this talk about sustainable development and the environment, events that accompanied the development of China and India have changed the nature of most issues and the magnitudes of economic, social, and environmental challenges we face. In fact, commitment to economic sustainability was undermined by the rapid change that characterized economic and social transformations in China and India. In the meantime, states in the West, with the exception of the United States, have accepted the science regarding the problems of air pollution and climate change and seem satisfied with what they are doing to meet both challenges. Economic development to be sustainable must seek to give people what they want without damaging the quality of the environment, especially in the developing world.

Environmental Sustainability

Environmental sustainability seeks to develop alternate sources of energy to conserve natural resources and reduce pollution and the harm caused to human, animal, and plant life. This requires replanting forests and protecting natural areas from resource extraction like mining and digging oil wells. However, in so doing, the protection of the environment is seen by most industries as undermining economic development; and this is the argument of many poor nations. Nevertheless, giving priority to economic sustainability can undermine efforts to protect the environment. So to be sustainable in the long run, Sustainability plans should take into consideration the three spheres of sustainability at the same time; ensuring the protection of the planet, sustaining economic development, and enhancing the welfare of people who are the hand that produces, the mouth that eats, the brain that plans and acts, and the creatures that inhabit the planet and share with the plants and animals the space they live in.

The Brundtland Commission Report, emphasizing the interdependence between man and nature stated that "The environment does not exist as a sphere separate from human actions, ambitions and needs, and therefore attempts to defend it in isolation from human concerns have given the very word environment a connotation of naivety in some political circles. The word development has also been narrowed by some into a very limited focus, along the lines of 'what poor nations should do to become richer.' But the environment is where we live; and development is what we all do in attempting to improve our lot within that abode. The two are inseparable."[11]

In 2007, a report written by Joy Hecht for the US Environmental Protection Agency stated, "Throughout the world, sustainability has become the common term for describing the objectives of public policy. Sustainability indicators have become a preferred tool for tracking the actions of public agencies. When these indicators move in the 'right' direction – if we even know what that is – does that really mean that our economy, our environment or our society is actually sustainable? Do we know how to define sustainability precisely enough to use it as a basis for assessing public policy decisions?"[12] But instead of trying to develop precise definitions, several states and UN agencies developed indicators which practitioners use to gauge the progress they are supposedly making. But how can anyone measure, for example, the progress that sustainable human development is making when the quality of education varies from one school to another, and from one country to another, and when cultural values and attitudes and patterns of consumption are not taken into consideration.

In the last 50 years, environmental sustainability efforts have improved the conditions of many lakes, rivers, and forests around the world, which means that "environmental sustainability seems to be moving on the right track toward achieving its objectives". However, other forms of sustainability appear to have failed to make tangible progress. After 50 years of publishing 'The Limits to Growth' and 35 years of issuing the Brundtland Commission Report, environmental indicators suggest that the world is not on the right track to either economic or social or cultural sustainability. According to reports issued by the United Nations, the World Bank, and several nongovernmental organizations, human rights and women's rights in particular are being violated systematically in many parts of the world; illiteracy rates are still high; the quality of education is declining in many states; poverty in spreading and becoming structural; and violence and discrimination are on the rise, especially in Europe and the United States.

The fact that sustainable development seeks to develop land and construct projects in ways that reduce the negative impact on the environment means that we should create energy efficient systems such as installing solar panels, building wind generators, and using geothermal heating techniques to produce the energy we need. The belief that the harm done in one area of the world can be counter balanced by preserving the environment somewhere else is based on a twisted view of the world that sees some people deserving more than others; the Chernobyl nuclear disaster of 1986 proved that this view is wrong and discriminatory.

> Environmental security emphasize that unsustainable human activities have resulted in environmental tribulations threatening life on Earth in various ways. These unsustainable activities have endangered the availability of critical resources, renewable as well as nonrenewable. For the sake of argument, let us consider three different scenarios that scarcity could possibly culminate into. First, it could trigger war for the control of inadequate resources resulting in 'resource capture' by few at the expense of 'ecological marginalization' of many. Secondly, it could provoke mass migration because of environmental suffering. Environmental refugees' adaptation in their new favorable habitation becomes very challenging, particularly in case of resistance from the host communities culminating in identity and or ethnic crises. And lastly, it could deteriorate socio-political institutions resulting in crisis of authority or civil disobedience.[13]

According to the Climate Risk Index 2015 prepared by German Watch between 1994 and 2013, more than 530,000 people have died worldwide and losses worth $2.17 trillion were inflicted as a direct result of over 15,000 extreme weather events. Water scarcity may also worsen and provoke military conflict. In the context of these multidimensional aspects of looming environmental problems, it is inevitable to look beyond the conventional national security parameters and consolidate the environmentalist version of security, which means that security must be considered a global issue. Therefore, "environmental protection is the need to protect the environment, whether the concept of 4 Rs (reduce, recycle, recover, and reuse) are being achieved or not. Environmental protection is the third pillar and, to many, the primary concern of the future of humanity. The aim of ecologically sustainable development is to maximize human well-being or quality of life without jeopardizing the life support system. The measures for sustainable development may be different in developed and developing countries according to their level of technological and economic development"[14]

Social Sustainability

Since the publishing of *The Limits to Growth*, people calling for the protection of the environment and others advocating free markets have called for reducing population growth rates to sustainable levels; they claim that such a reduction is necessary to preventing the human race from destroying the planetary support systems. But what is the population growth rate that is sustainable? No one seems to know. Improving the productivity of all forms of capital and substituting knowledge for other factors of production have enabled our planet to support more people than ever imagined, making projections of sustainable population growth rates hard to come by. In 2022 the world population reached 8 billion, the population of China declined, and the world population growth rate declined to less than 1% after peaking at 2.2% in 1963. Due to the spread of education and the accessibility of information regarding most aspects of life, and the need of most couples to work, rates of population growth have declined substantially. World population is currently (2023) growing at 0.88% per year. Though the world population is expected to grow throughout the twenty-first century, the rate of growth will be very slow compared to the recent past.[15]

Since the current rate of growth is less than 1% annually, I believe that expected improvements in technology alone can take care of the increase in population without having to use more natural resources. In fact, as technology advances and new, more efficient tools and systems are invented, the productivity of labor, capital, and land increases, making it possible to produce larger amounts of goods and services by using the same amount of inputs. Technology is also making it possible to make all goods and services we produce better, safer, less expensive, and more durable, while reducing the cost of production in terms of time, manpower, and money.

The 17 sustainable development goals adopted by the United Nations in 2015 recognize "that eradicating poverty in all its forms and dimensions, including extreme poverty, is the greatest global challenge and an indispensable requirement for sustainable development." But with regimes that violate the rights of their citizens and foreign powers that corrupt politicians and compel them to steal the resources of their nations to purchase arms, no social development would be achieved. In fact, Western powers, especially the United States, Britain, and France are selling arms to dictators of poor nations and using covert operations to destroy indigenous cultures and dismantle the social and cultural fabrics of societies. As a consequence no social sustainability is possible and no environmental or economic sustainability is likely to be accomplished. This is why nothing of value has been accomplished in either economic or social or environmental sustainability in almost all poor societies.

It is estimated that achieving the sustainable development goals needs to mobilize $5 to 7 trillion per year, which is not possible now or in the future. However, the Ramo Plan to liberate all rich and poor nations from the debt burden—to be outlined and explained later in Chapter 15—saves all concerned states about $4 to 5 trillion annually in interest payment on the current debt, making the targeted goals within reach without having to worry about mobilizing tons of money. The Ramo plan is the only known strategy to pave the way for global sustainable development, promote peace, and create millions of investment opportunities for all rich nations and corporations to benefit from, because it ties the interests of all parties together; reduces competition among the great powers; undermines the incentive to launch wars; and saves the social and cultural fabrics of poor societies.

Nevertheless, the world's poor need more healthy food to eat, while the world's rich need to eat less and stop wasting food and other things, and corporations need to stop wasting human and natural resources by producing harmful products like cigarettes and cancerous chemicals. This means that the cultures of conspicuous consumption and waste by individuals and corporations need to become less wasteful and more conserving. The Brundtland Report says, "Sustainable development involves more than growth. It requires a change in the content of growth, to make it less material and energy intensive and more equitable in its impact. These changes are required in all countries as part of a package of measures to maintain the stock of ecological capital, to improve the distribution of income, and to reduce the degree of vulnerability to economic crises."[16]

Social development needs to make people aware of their rights and how to stay healthy, which requires new laws to protect the health of people from pollution and the harmful activities of business. Awareness should encourage people to participate in the economic, social, and environmental sustainability activities, and teach them about the benefits of environmental protection, while warning them of the dangers of neglecting their social responsibilities. Social sustainability should also aim at accomplishing universal primary education and health care, with particular emphasis on the education and social liberation of women.

In September 2000, 189 member states of the UN came together at the Millennium Summit and adopted the Millennium Declaration, which emphasized the role of values in human life. The declaration stated, "We consider certain fundamental values to be essential to international relations in the twenty-first century." These fundamental values include:

1. Freedom. Men and women have the right to live their lives and raise their children in dignity, free from hunger and the fear of violence, oppression or injustice. Democratic and participatory governance based on the will of the people best assures these rights.
2. Equality. No individual and no nation must be denied the opportunity to benefit from development. The equal rights and opportunities of women and men must be assured.
3. Solidarity. Global challenges must be managed in a way that distributes the costs and burdens fairly in accordance with basic principles of equity and social justice. Those who suffer or who benefit least deserve help from those who benefit most.
4. Tolerance. Human beings must respect one other. Differences within and between societies should be neither feared nor repressed but cherished as a precious asset of humanity. A culture of peace and dialogue among all civilizations should be promoted.
5. Respect for nature. "Prudence must be shown in the management of all living species and natural resources, in accordance with the precepts of sustainable development. Only in this way can the immeasurable riches provided to us by nature be preserved and passed on to our descendants. The current unsustainable patterns of production and consumption must be changed in the interest of our future welfare and that of our descendants."[17]

Since no individual can survive by himself, no system can function without other systems. Therefore it is not possible to achieve any goal without the active cooperation of peoples, states, business, and civil society organizations; and for such cooperation to exist the relationships between the many entities must be based on trust and sharing the benefits and sacrifices, which current economic and military competition make it rather impossible to achieve. In fact, almost ten years after this declaration, the situation has worsened everywhere. This makes social sustainability a priority, if not the main pillar of sustainability. Peoples, states, business entities, organizations, and interests are intertwined, and for any meaningful action to be achieved, all these components have to cooperate within a framework that recognizes that the objective is to create a just global society for all.

Sustainable development involves the pursuit of environmental quality, economic prosperity, human development, social equity, freedom, and cultural diversity. If pursued as such, sustainable development would be able to protect the environment, enable all people to meet their basic needs, achieve social justice and peace, and liberate women and men from political and cultural chains that undermine their potentials. It should also undermine the capacity of corporations and some states to use the sustainability issue to protect their interests while preventing poor nations from developing their economies. Therefore, the way to achieve sustainability is to integrate economic, environmental, social policies, cultural values, the development of human resources, and education together.

Understanding the relationship between human actions and environmental changes is essential to managing our natural resources and achieving our economic and social goals. Human actions cause climate change, and climate change affects both economies and societies. Natural catastrophes like storms, floods and droughts, and earthquakes, make habitation in affected areas hard to sustain. According to the World Bank, "By 2050, it could mean that as many as 143 million people across three developing regions will become climate migrants, with individuals, families and whole communities forced to seek more viable and less vulnerable places to live in."[18]

Human mobility is caused by environmental change, political repression, poverty, lack of freedom and opportunity, and conflict and war. This is where the link between social and environmental sustainability comes into play. As environments worsen, humans suffer the consequences of their actions and future generations pay the price. Unfortunately, the ruling elites of the major powers that stand behind wars, and corporations that contribute to climate change escape the punishment, some actually benefit from such catastrophes at the expense of their nations and the poor of the world.

Since one of the major goals of sustainable development is to put people first, the way to achieve this goal presents an obstacle to reaching an international consensus on sustainability. Different nations tend to view human rights differently; and needs and expectations of people vary greatly from state to state, according to their cultures and levels of development. In fact, one nation's needs could be another nation's luxuries. Helen Clark, administrator of the United Nations Development Program, said in 2012, "If the way in which both rich and poor nations develop is destructive of the very ecosystems on which life on this planet depends, then the burden will fall disproportionately on the poorest and most vulnerable people who depend the most on healthy ecosystems for their survival and have the least means to adapt to the challenges brought by environmental degradation."[19]

As national development agencies strive to achieve sustainability, they tend to treat it as a largely national rather than global endeavor. But the three major categories of sustainability—economic, environment, and social—cannot be attained except at the global level, because many nations have access to nonrenewable resources like water and natural gas to waste, and rivers and seas to pollute without giving much consideration to the needs and interests of other nations that depend on the same resources. In addition, the flood of immigrants from conflict-ridden poor states to the West cannot be stopped without helping those states develop and be stable. Poverty, political and economic corruption, and American intervention in the national affairs of many states, especially in the Middle East and Latin America have triggered one of the largest waves of immigration in recent history.

This migration reflects the social dimension of sustainability that has become a hotly debated issue in Europe and America, causing the social fabric of societies to be undermined, not only the ones that suffer poverty and conflict, but also Western societies in general. Therefore, fairness and reality dictate that sustainability must be treated as a global endeavor; sacrifices needed to accomplish it; and benefits generated by it should be shared by all nations. "In order to be sustainable, development must also be harmonious. At least a certain amount of social cohesion must exist on a planetary scale in order to create the conditions for the peace we need."[20]

Since all these issues are global, the only development that could be sustainable is global development that makes national changes an integral part of a global grand design. Because every major change touches the lives of everyone in society, the process of sustainable development cannot succeed unless we understand it and manage it as a participatory process. Every member of the world community must feel that he and she has a stake in change, and a vital role to play in making change. The Chinese experience proves that public projects that fail to get people involved in designing them are more likely to anger people and fail. The demonstrations which Shanghai witnessed in the summer of 2012 suggest that economic growth that damages the environment degrades rather than upgrades the quality of life and makes money worthless.

Before concluding this chapter, we should recognize that war and conflict, and great economic and military powers competition with each other, and their aggressive interference in the affairs of struggling poor nations, work to undermine all efforts to achieve sustainability, and cause bad situations to get worse. What happened since 2003 in Iraq, Libya, Sudan, Syria, Yemen, and several African, Asian, and Latin American countries proves this point; the wars that were instigated and aggrieved by the great powers have caused millions of causalities and millions of refugees to lose their homes and leave their countries. As the peoples of poor countries became disparate, racism has become uglier and more aggressive, particularly in the United States, Britain, and France, causing these societies to become less socially sustainable.

Notes

1. Donovan Finn, *Our Uncertain Future: Can Good Planning Create Sustainable Communities?* University of Illinois, 2009, 3.
2. World Commission on Environment and Development, *Our Common Future*, Chapter 2, http://www.un-documents.net/ocf-02.htm.
3. Michael Thomas Needham, A Psychological Approach to a Thriving Resilient Community, *International Journal of Business, Humanities and Technology*, vol. 1, No. 3, November 2011.
4. Towards Sustainable Development, *Our Common Future*, www.un-documents.net.

5. http://www.legrand.com/EN/sustainable-development-description_12847.html.
6. Robert W. Kates, Thomas M Parris, and Anthony A. Leiserowitz, What is Sustainable Development? *Environment: Science and Policy for Sustainable Development*, vol. 47, No. 3, April 2005, 9.
7. unesco.org/en/ev.php-URL_ID 13,179&URL_DO=DO_TOPIC&URL_SECTION=201.html.
8. http://www.legrand.com/EN/sustainable-development-description_12847.html.
9. Ibid.
10. See Mohamed Rabie; *A Theory of Sustainable Sociocultural and Economic Development,* Palgrave Macmillan, 2016, 17–31.
11. Chairman's forward, Our Common Future, http://www.un-documents.net/wced-ocf.htm.
12. Joy E. Hecht, Can Indicators and Accounts Really Measure Sustainability? Considerations for the U.S. Environmental Protection Agency, www.scribd.com.
13. https://www.essay.uk.com/essays/environmental-studies/environmental-security/.
14. Ibid.
15. Worldmeters, https://www.worldometers.info/world-population/.
16. Toward Sustainable Development, *Our Common Future*, www.un-documents.net.
17. United Nations General Assembly, "United Nations Millennium Declaration," Resolution 55/2, United Nations A/RES/55/2, 18 September 2000, page x.
18. World Bank, Climate Change, https://www.worldbank.org/en/topic/climatechange/overview.
19. Helen Clark, Achieving Sustainable Human Development, May 29, 2012, https://www.undp.org/content/undp/en/home/presscenter/speeches/2012/05/29/helen-clark-achieving-sustainable-human-development-.html.
20. http://www.legrand.com/EN/sustainable-development-description_12847.html.

CHAPTER 14

The Global Refugee Crisis

Abstract This chapter seeks to end the global refugee crisis in a human way that rewards all involved parties and punishes no one. The parties that are being asked to get involved in ending this crisis are the United States and the European Community members. The tool created to deal with this human tragedy is the envisioned MoRa Plan that asks the America and European states to finance a program to economically develop the Latin American, the Middle Eastern, and the African countries over a period of 20 years. Today, poor immigrants arriving from Latin America at the borders of the United States daily and waves of desperate refugees arriving at the shores of Europe on ships that caused the drowning of thousands of refugees since 2011, have created a backlash in Europe and America. Resistance to accommodating disparate refugees fleeing war, poverty, and violence has caused tolerance, compassion, and empathy in Europe and America to decline, and caused racism, discrimination, and hate to rise and undermine the democratic system in both continents. Though there is no doubt that widespread political and economic corruption, high unemployment rates, and lack of freedom in most Latin American, Middle Eastern, African, and Asian countries are major causes of this human tragedy, there is also no doubt that the colonialist policies and the imperialistic ambitions of America and other European states were major forces that caused this tragic situation in the first place.

M. Rabie, *A Future Economy for All*,
https://doi.org/10.1007/978-3-031-42957-6_14

Keywords Foreign interference · Colonial powers · Britain · France · Belgium · Portugal · Spain · Italy · Holland Socialism · Democracy · Drug and human trafficking · Civil Wars · Ghosts · Criminal gangs

Poor immigrants arriving from Latin America at the borders of the United States daily and waves of desperate refugees arriving at the shores of Europe have created a backlash in both continents. Resistance to refugees fleeing war, poverty, and violence has caused tolerance, compassion, and empathy in Europe and America to decline, and caused racism, discrimination, and hate to rise and undermine the efficiency of the democratic system in both continents. There is no doubt that widespread political and economic corruption, high unemployment rates, and lack of freedom in most Latin American, Middle Eastern, African, and Asian countries are major causes of this human tragedy that seems to have no end in sight. But there is also no doubt that the colonialist policies and the imperialistic ambitions of America and other European states were major forces that caused this tragic situation in the first place. American and European corrupt leaders, divided peoples and created fertile environments for the rich and powerful to exploit the poor and subordinate the weak, ignore education and the need to develop the national economies.

In the meantime, continued foreign interference in the affairs of poor states gave both the people and the ruling elites of these states a reason to blame the other for their utter failure. There are many cases where the colonial powers stole the natural resources of the colonized peoples, and intentionally hindered their efforts to develop their economies and move toward democracy. The British and French are responsible for most of the damage caused to most Middle Eastern and African countries; Britain, France, Belgium, and Portugal stole the natural resources of many poor African nations, undermined the capacity of their economies to grow, and empowered corrupt dictators to suppress the masses and destroy their aspirations for freedom and economic development.

In Latin America, the United States occupied many states, some of them several times, it also cultivated and armed gangs, some directly and others indirectly, to fight socialism and undermine democracy, and that paved the way for drug and human trafficking gangs to grow and flourish. Several horrendous stories can be told, where Britain and France intervened to create chaos and prolong civil conflicts, kill teachers, destroy villages, and sell arms to criminals to achieve long-term strategic goals at the expense of the poor natives.

However, the purpose of this proposal is not to condemn certain states or ask for apologies or restitution, but to ask the US and the EU states to correct the moral mistakes they made in the past. The actions of the British, French, Belgium, Spanish, Portuguese, Dutch, Italian, and American ruling elites over the last two centuries have created ghosts that are now coming back to haunt them, and revive racism, hatred, and extremism at home. The need today is not to blame each other and find excuses, but to curb the tides of immigrants, stop the waves of refugees, save nameless children from raging seas, and free enslaved girls and boys from the grip of criminal gangs.

According to the America Immigration Council, "currently, the number of border and interior enforcement officers stands at more than 50,000, with CBP (U.S. Customs and Border Protection) and ICE (U.S. Immigration and Customs Enforcement) employing together over 84,000 people. In February 2019, Congress reached a deal with the President, offering S1.375 billion for 55 miles of fencing, but the president, shortly after signing the bill, declared a national emergency to fund his border wall through other means. In addition to the $1.375 billion, he pulled much more money from the budgets of other departments, totaling 8.2 billion. Nevertheless, all this spending in the name of security has failed to make the border more secure. The border patrol budget has increased more than tenfold, from $363 million in 2003 to nearly $4.9 billion in 2021. CBP budget has also nearly tripled, rising from $5.9 billion in 2003 to $17.7 billion in 2021. In addition, the ICE detention beds rose from 34,000 to 40,000 in 2018 to 55,000 people in 2019".[1]

Since 1993,has more than doubled, rising from $5.9 billion the number of US Border Patrol agents has skyrocketed from 4139 agents to 19,648 agents in 2019. In addition, 2073 agents are deployed to the US-Canada border, and 255 agents are deployed to the coastal border sectors. The number of the CBP officers staffing ports of entry grew from 17,279 in 2003 to 24,511 in 2019. The number of ICE agents grew from 2710 in 2003 to 6201 in 2019. In total, ICE employs more than 20,000 people. The American Immigration Council (AIC) says that "Since the creation of the Department of Homeland Security (DHS) in 2003, the federal government has spent an estimated $333 billion on the agencies that carry out immigration enforcement… since 1993, the annual budget of the US Border Patrol has increased more than ten-fold, from $363 million to more than $4.7 billion." The AIC says further that "since the creation of DHS, ICE spending has grown 103%, from $3.3 billion to $6.7 billion. Much of this funding has gone to increasing the agency's ability to hold immigrants in detention in locations around the country. Meanwhile, the CBP budget has more than doubled, rising from $5.9 billion in 2003 to $14.7 billion in 2019".[2] In addition, the US Congress approved an additional $4.6 billion at the end of June 2019 to deal with the humanitarian crises at America's borders. As for the DHS budget, the Congressional Research Service (CRS) says that the 2019 budget was $62.178 billion; and when the new appropriation is added, the total would be $66.8 billion. However, there are thousands more fighting to end the activities of ICE.

Though the old immigration policy has failed, the Trump policy revived racism and violence in America, while making ideological polarization worse than ever before. The Biden administration has increased the number of victims of America's immigration procedures. To ease this crisis, some people are calling for increasing financial aid to the Latin American states from which the bulk of refugees come. But such a policy is like a band-aid; it may reduce the pain temporarily, but it cannot cure a disease whose roots are of socioeconomic and sociopolitical nature.

The MoRa Plan

To deal with the current global refugee crisis in a comprehensive and humane manner, it is suggested that America commit to spending $2 trillion to develop Latin American states and help their peoples transform their cultures and economies. It is further suggested that money be spent over 20 years, $100 billion annually. Europeans should do the same by committing to spend 2 trillion Euros over 20 years to develop the economies of Middle Eastern, and African countries and help their peoples to develop their economies, transform their cultures, and move toward democracy.

All States of Western Europe need to share financing the MoRa plan to protect their borders from the waves of economic and war refugees and undermine the forces of racism and radicalism in Europe. I believe that this is the only way for European leaders to save their cultural values, maintain civility at home, undermine radicalism and terrorism abroad, and revitalize their struggling economies and frustrated populations.

It is suggested that the United States, the eurozone states, and Britain create the money needed to finance the MoRa programs instead of borrowing the money. Most sites say that the amount of US dollars circulating were about $6 trillion in 2020. As for the Euros, it was about 8.1 trillion, making the total dollars, Euros, and British Pounds about 16 trillion. So, adding $200 billion annually amounts to increasing the money supply by less than two-tenth of one percent. This means that the money to be created to finance the MoRa programs would have no effect on the global supply of money.

Western states in general and the United States in particular claim to give a lot of money to poor nations, and they do. But estimates of money going from the poor states to the rich ones are said to be many times what the rich give to the poor. In 2017, the Guardian published an article explaining this issue: information is based on a report issued by the Global Financial Integrity and the Centre for Applied Research at the Norwegian School of Economics in Norway. According to the report, "the flow of money from rich countries to poor countries pales in comparison to the flow that runs in the other direction. In 2012, the last year of recorded data, developing countries received a total of $1.3 trillion, including all aid, investment, and income from abroad".[3]

In contrast, some $3.3 trillion were transferred from the developing countries to the rich ones. "In other words, developing countries sent $2 trillion more to the rest of the world than they received. If we look at all years since 1980, these net outflows add up to an eye-popping total of $16.3 trillion. What this means is that the usual development narrative has it backward. Aid is effectively flowing in reverse. Rich countries aren't developing poor countries; poor countries are developing rich ones."[4] This means that even if Western states were to borrow the money and spend $200 billion annually to finance the MoRa programs, the West would be returning to the developing countries about 10% of what it receives from them each year.

It is further suggested that the MoRa programs be engaged in six areas; first, infrastructure building that includes roads, ports, and airports; second, housing for the poor and low-income families; third, technical training in high schools using the German model; forth, healthcare using the Kaiser Permanente model developed in America; fifth, tourism training that includes environmental preservation and revival of traditional handcraft industries; and sixth, raising agricultural productivity.

However, for the MoRa programs to succeed, four steps need to be taken simultaneously:

1. The formation of an International Anti-Crime Task Force (ICTF) to hunt gangs involved in drug trade and violence and human trafficking and bring them to justice; a $4 billion annual budget, to be paid by the Latin and Middle Eastern programs would be allocated to this force. However, it is suggested that members of all criminal gangs be offered amnesty and the opportunity to live in America, in exchange for giving ICTF full account of their crimes and the names of their accomplices and how they moved their money around; and submit to a two-year rehabilitation program to prepare them to lead normal lives in their new homeland.
2. Since economic development and social plans take time to start creating jobs for the unemployed and housing for the poor, 70% of the MoRa budget should be distributed in cash in the first year; this cash portion would be reduced by 10% annually. After 10 years, all funds would be invested in the economic, social, cultural, and educational programs.
3. No program of this nature can succeed and be sustained without uprooting political and economic corruption. To start with, the United Nations should declare that political and economic corruption is a crime under the international human rights law, and set a special court, in cooperation with ICTF to bring violators to justice. Nations that refuse to abide by this law should be barred from membership in all international organizations, including the UN, and denied access to outside financial sources.
4. The UN, to put all nations and ruling elites on the path to civility, should demand that constitutions of all states limit the office terms of president and prime minister to a maximum of 10 years, and transform all kingdoms to constitutional monarchies within a specified time; freedom of people must have priority over the freedom of corrupt politicians and cruel dictators.

I believe that in a few months of starting the cash program, the number of immigrants and refugees to America and Europe will start declining, reaching probably half of its current size by the end of the second year. The United States should save about $4 billion of the CBP and ICE budgets in the first year, and about 50% by the end of the third year. No person would normally take the risk of leaving his family and country if he has an opportunity to live a dignified life at home. By the middle of this program, the social, cultural, political, and economic landscapes of all nations involved would be transformed to become peaceful and clean backyards for Americans and Europeans to visit, get a taste of genuine cultures, and live moments in an enchanting past.

Markets of these countries would grow and diversify to absorb much of the West's exports, enabling Western economies to grow and flourish. Before the MoRa programs end, the West should have made at least $4 to $5 trillion in profits, because Western companies would carry out most of the work needed to build the infrastructure, modernize agriculture, build homes for the poor, and industrialize those countries. If each $5000 in spending and investing were to create one job, each program would create 20 million jobs annually. In the meantime, private investment from national and foreign sources should increase fast, causing each program to create 600–700 million jobs over 20 years, and thus end unemployment in Latin American and Middle Eastern and African countries.

To recognize the magnitude of the benefits that would accrue to the West due to the MoRa plan, we need to look at the size of the combined economies and populations of both groups. In 2019, the total population of the Arab, African, and Latin American countries was about 2 billion, and their combined GDPs were about $13 trillion in 2021. Assuming that the economies of those countries will grow by 6% annually during the implementation of the MoRa plan, their combined GDP would reach $40 trillion in 20 years, creating a Western friendly market about $3 trillion larger than the 2021 GDPs of the United States, Germany, Britain, France, Canada, and Italy combined. This should cause the export markets for the European and American companies in Latin America, Africa, and the Middle East to triple in 20 years.

Since the money required to finance the MoRa programs would be created rather than borrowed, no state or taxpayer would pay anything. Adopting these costless programs is the only option the West has to maintain its prominent world economic and political status and reset its damaged relationship with its victims while reviving its economies and expanding its export markets. If this were to happen, it might encourage Japan, China, South Korea, and India to do something similar in Asia and enable Pakistan, Bangladesh, Afghanistan, Laos, Cambodia,

Nepal, Myanmar, the Philippines, and other Asian nations to develop and become stable and peaceful.

Americans and Europeans need to be reminded that the center of global economic power is shifting fast from the West to the East, taking with it research centers, and creating great scientific and military power, particularly in China. Therefore the West has no time to waste. This makes the MoRa plan the West's option to save itself from racism, hatred, and violence at home, and strengthen its political, economic, and military position abroad.

If helping poor nations was a luxury in the past, it is a global security and human necessity today. World political stability cannot be sustained, and radicalism cannot be contained without economic development and a fairer distribution of wealth among social classes and nations. Financial aid can buy corrupt leaders but cannot create enough jobs for the unemployed. Money alone can neither feed hungry children nor stem the rising tide of racism and hatred in the West. Since our world has become a global village, no nation can live in peace for long unless other nations feel at peace as well. No nation can feel financially and economically comfortable and politically stable unless its friends and enemies feel the same; and no nation will feel secure unless its neighbors feel secure as well.

One half of 1% of the money created to finance the MoRa programs would go to Prof. Rabie who conceived this idea and articulated the MoRa plan. In return, Rabie commits to donating 99.5% of this money to establish a global foundation to be called the "Peace and Development Foundation" (PDF), and the "Institute for Creative Ideas" (ICI); ICI would guide the work of PDF, which aims to promote peace and sociocultural transformation; grow the local and regional capacities to solve conflict peacefully; empower the poor and weak, with emphasis on women; discover and develop young people's talents; fight homelessness and poverty; train young people how to think critically and rationally and stay away from violence and radicalism; and encourage reading to eliminate cultural illiteracy in the less developed countries.

In the following chapter, a plan is articulated to end the global debt problem and free all nations from the debt burden; the plan also provides for the establishment of four multi-trillion dollar funds to address the issues of helping the victims of natural disasters, preserving the environment, improving education, and developing the economies of poor nations. Half of 1% of the money allocated to finance these funds will be treated just like the money allocated to finance the Peace and Development Foundation and the Institute for Creative Ideas.

Notes

1. The Cost of Immigration Enforcement and Border Security, American Immigration Council, October 2019, https://www.americanimmigrationcouncil.org/sites/default/files/research/the_cost_of_immigration_enforcement_and_border_security.pdf.
2. Ibid.
3. Jason Hickel; Aid in Reverse: How Poor Countries Develop Rich Countries; The Guardian, January 14, 2017, https://www.theguardian.com/global-development-professionals-network/2017/jan/14/aid-in-reverse-how-poor-countries-develop-rich-countries.
4. Ibid.

CHAPTER 15

The Ramo Plan

Abstract The Ramo Plan is a visionary proposal to liberate all rich and poor nations from the burden of debt, it tries to expose the magnitude of the global debt problem, what caused it, how to deal with it, and why we need to liberate all nations from the debt burden now. The analyses and discussion place the debt issue in its proper historical and social contexts and answer the questions that could be raised against it. The plan was published by Ideas, a website of the German Munich University, and US Federal Reserve Bank of St. Louis. However, the plan went through several stages of development that forced me to spend many sleepless nights thinking how to structure it, what projects should be included in it, and how to finance its grandiose projects and achieve the desired humanitarian goals. All of which are identified and explained in this chapter.

Keywords 2008 Financial Crisis · Greece · Ireland · Portugal · Public Debt · International Monetary Fund · Taxpayers · Bondholders · Globalization · South Korea · China · India · Brazil · Pakistan · Egypt · Economic Theory · Bloomberg · Dollars · Euros · Pounds · Sustainable Development Fund · Educational Fund · Humanitarian Fund · Environmental Fund · Helicopter money

M. Rabie, *A Future Economy for All*,
https://doi.org/10.1007/978-3-031-42957-6_15

The Ramo Plan is a visionary proposal to liberate all rich and poor nations from the burden of debt. The plan tries to expose the magnitude of the debt problem, what caused it and how to deal with it while explaining why we need to liberate all nations from the debt burden now. Therefore, the discussion places the debt issue in its proper historical and social contexts and answers the questions that could be raised against it. The plan was published by Ideas, a website of the German Munich University, and US Federal Reserve Bank of St. Louis. However, the Ramo plan went through several stages of developments that forced me to spend many sleepless nights thinking how to structure it, what projects should be included in it, and how to finance its grandiose projects The following analysis explains why over half of the world's states can never repay their debt under current circumstances and how to deal with the debt problem.

Due to the financial crisis of 2008, many states were forced to bail out troubled banks and failing corporations by adopting expansionist policies to stimulate their sagging economies. Consequently, borrowing to cover spending increased substantially, causing budget deficits and the public debt of most nations to rise rapidly and reach, in many cases, unsustainable levels. In view of the near default of Greece, Ireland, and Portugal, global awareness of the threat posed by growing public debt was heightened, giving rise to a eurozone crisis. Today, many states are facing a dilemma: how to reduce budget deficits to contain rising public debts on the one hand, and how to grow their economies to create jobs for the unemployed on the other.

All indebted nations subscribing to the free market system are in a bind; the goals they seek to accomplish are contradictory, and the actions they must take are incompatible. While reducing deficits to contain the increasing debt requires reducing spending and raising taxes, stimulating slow growing economies, and creating jobs require more spending and tax reductions. Since there is no formula in economic books to achieve these contradictory goals, a new formula has to be invented to enable nations to resume healthy economic growth and create millions of new jobs without widening deficits or increasing the public debt.

The Ramo Plan provides a way to liberate all nations from the debt burden, restructure the international monetary system, and create the necessary conditions for sustainable global sociocultural and economic development while guaranteeing fairness and protecting of the environment. The plan has come as a result of deep thinking about the woes of our times; the duty to help poor people and desperate children climb out of poverty; the need to save students from debt and inadequate education; and a moral responsibility to liberate oppressed young women and men from economic and social enslavement. The plan also aims to free future generations from the burden of debt incurred by previous generations. Since the intention is to help everyone, the plan neither asks investors nor bondholders nor banks nor taxpayers to sacrifice anything nor calls for the redistribution of wealth; it is designed to help everyone and penalizes no one.

But before outlining the plan, a few facts related to global change need to be underlined. Analyzing these facts is meant to place the major economic challenges of our times in their proper historical and societal contexts; otherwise, it would be difficult for most people to understand the nature and extent of global change and its strategic implications.

Global Context of Change

"**Globalization** and the communications and information revolutions and technological innovations of the last three decades have caused national economies, cultures, and politics to be transformed; they created a global economy that forced economic and social structures and production relations to change, causing the nation state to lose control over its economy. They also caused most industrialized societies to enter a transitional period leading to a new, much complex civilization, having its own society, culture, and economy. During transitional periods that take societies from one civilization to another, it is always easier to describe change than identify its causes, influence its course, or predict its outcome. As change proceeds, it invalidates prevailing economic, social, and political theories, while no new ones are developed in time to take the place of the old ones and deal with the evolving consequences of change. They also cause confusion, chaos and create a trust deficit".[1] And this causes the capacity of society to deal with the new reality to decline, creating a need for new ideas and laws and theories to guide nations into a largely uncharted future no one can escape.

The transition that started in most Western states around the mid-1990s has disrupted life as we knew it; it dissolved the connection between the immediate past and the near future, causing most people to lose their sense of direction. But as the industrial was about to reach its end, the knowledge age was still in labor being born, leaving the present waiting for the unknown. The present we were living then was reduced to a mere port where the past is ending its journey, while the future is getting ready to start its voyage into a new world. Consequently, people and the systems through which they function are experiencing one crisis after another without much hope of regaining balance soon. In fact, the moment a civilizational era ends, its history and historical logic end, forcing the new era to struggle alone to discover the logic of its times and write its own history. For example, when the Industrial Revolution arrived with its unique society, culture, and economy in the second half of the eighteenth century, the history of the agricultural era and its logic ended, causing that history to lose its wisdom, and become of little use to the new society and the unfolding new age.

The rapid industrialization of South Korea, China, India, Brazil, and other states has caused the global capacity to produce most essential goods and services to exceed the global capacity to absorb such goods and services. Meanwhile, the continued expansion of this capacity has caused competition to intensify and the global economic growth rates to decline. While exposing the world economy to recessions and financial crises, it created a need to expand global markets to keep pace with the growing production capacity. Since the absorption capacity of the industrial states is fast approaching its limits, due in part to the shrinking size of the middle class, aging populations, and an ever-widening gap between rich and poor, efforts to develop new markets must concentrate on poor countries where economies are still underdeveloped, and people are hungry for everything new.

Some people might argue, correctly, that instead of expanding markets we should reduce the production capacity of countries like China to conserve our dwindling natural resources and protect our environment. Though this is a rational argument, it is not practical at this turn in history; many millions of young people are still unemployed and struggling to survive in India, Pakistan, Egypt, and tens of other Asia, Africa, and Latin America states. While we should strive to conserve as much of our natural resources as possible, we need first to create jobs for the world's unemployed men and women to guarantee fairness; however, we should never lose sight of the need to protect our environment.

Free trade and investment markets have changed the rules that govern many things in life, particularly rules that govern the relationships between jobs and jobseekers. Three decades or so ago, many jobseekers had to leave their towns and families, sometimes their countries, and risk dying to reach a country where decent jobs are available to help them improve their living conditions. While economic migration continues today, most immigrants lack the skills needed to excel in the new knowledge-based economy. Thousands of people die each year trying to reach Europe and the United States in little boats sailing against turbulent winds and walking across vast deserts controlled by criminals, human traffickers, and drug dealers.

Today, while industrial jobs travel from one country to another looking for cheap and disciplined labor that has the right skills and attitudes to hire, knowledge jobs travel, often virtually, looking for workers with the right education and talents. Since multinational corporations have abandoned their commitments to labor, community, and country, they are willing to hire anyone and invest in any country to maximize profits and enlarge market share. Therefore, highly qualified people do not need to leave their towns to get good jobs with corporations residing in faraway places.

These developments have caused most economic, social, and cultural conditions and structures to change drastically and irreversibly; as a result, they have invalidated most of the assumptions upon which old theories of economic and financial management are based. Such assumptions include the notions that national economies are largely closed, trade is subject to restrictions, foreign investment is subject to regulations, investment requires domestic savings, neither labor nor money is free to cross state lines without approval, and that the state is in control of its economy. Since all such restrictions have been fully or partially removed, the traditional tools of managing national economies and dealing with issues such as recessions, unemployment, inflation, and trade, have become ineffective, causing the **traditional economic theory** to become largely dysfunctional. Failure to acknowledge the declining relevance of traditional economic theory will cause most economists and politicians to think inside a largely empty box and fail to realize the need for new tools of economic and financial management.

There is no doubt that traditional economic thinking has had a solid record of success between the 1950s and the 1980s. Economists played and continue to play a major role debating economic policy, political decisions, the distribution of income and wealth, and the impact of these issues on fairness, poverty, the middle class, and the general welfare of nations. However, the moment a theory loses the validity of its assumptions, it loses its relevance and becomes dysfunctional. Building a theory is similar to building a house; you start with the foundations, which is the equivalent of assumptions for theory. If the foundations are good, the house will last for a long time, but not forever. Nevertheless, foundations exposed to earthquakes or floods are unlikely to live long; and so are assumptions trying to reflect human behavior and living conditions that never stop evolving and changing.

Overview of the Debt Problem

According to a report issued by the International Monetary Fund, 2020 witnessed "the largest one-year debt surge since World War II, with global debt rising to $226 trillion as the world was hit by a global health crisis and a deep recession. Debt was already elevated going into the crisis, but now governments must navigate a world of record-high public and private debt levels, new virus mutations, and rising inflation. Global debt rose by 28 percentage points to 256% of GDP in 2020, according to the latest update of the IMF's Global Debt Database. Debt increases are particularly striking in advanced economies, where public debt rose from around 70 percent of GDP in 2007, to 124 percent of GDP in 2020. Private debt, on the other hand, rose from 164 to 178% of GDP, in the same period."[2]

Without going into details, public records indicate that we have today 86 countries whose debt to GDP exceeds 60%. 24 of these countries have public debts to GDP that exceed 100%; they include the United States with a public debt to GDP of 137%, Japan (266), Greece (193), Italy (151), Portugal (127), Canada (118), Spain (118), and France (113). This means that we have a total of 86 countries that cannot repay their debt anytime in the future. Most of these figures are for 2020, which means that the impact of COVID-19 and the Ukraine crisis have not been considered.[3] It is estimated that the public debt increased by $20 trillion since the COVID-19 pandemic, making the total debt about $92 trillion, of which about 80% is owned by the Western industrialized states and Japan

However, I believe that when all states reveal their actual debt obligations, the total will most likely exceed $120 trillion. According to Bloomberg, the total public and private and corporate debt reached $250 trillion in 2019. "The world now has $250 trillion in global debt and growing. More importantly, global debt as a percentage of GDP climbed from just over 280% to nearly 320% over the past decade. There's simply too much debt in the system and no clear path to truly paying it off."[4]

In addition, the Economist said that global debt was approaching $300 trillion.

The Ramo Plan

Today, most nations face mountains of debt and huge budget deficits that hinder their abilities to grow their economies, create jobs for the unemployed, or help the poor and students burdened by debt. As a result, poverty and unemployment rates have remained high in most countries, and a sense of hopelessness and helplessness overwhelms a majority of people in many parts of the world. Since the debt problem is not limited to several states, it must be viewed as a global issue. To address this issue and the serious social ills it has precipitated, I present below the "Ramo Plan," which is a creative idea that defies conventional economic thinking; yet it has the capacity to liberate all states from the debt burden, restructure the international monetary system, restore global financial stability, and create the necessary conditions for sustainable global development and peace. The plan is as follows:

1. To designate the International Monetary Fund (IMF) a global central bank, with powers to issue a new international currency to be called "Ramo," divided into 100 cents, and to issue bonds in Ramos in addition to its current functions.
2. To set the value of the Ramo at the rate of the IMF Special Drawing Rights unit, which means converting the virtual IMF currency to a real one that can be used by everyone.
3. To give each state the opportunity to repay its entire debt obligations by issuing money notes and credit certificates in its own national currency payable to the IMF.
4. To authorize the IMF to open a trust account in which all such funds would be deposited and kept for the sole purpose of meeting the debt obligations of the IMF member states, the IMF would pay all debt notes on behalf of its members as they become due, not before or after.
5. To ask each state to pay an additional amount equal to 10% of its total debt obligations as management fees; these fees, expected to be about $12 trillion, would be deposited in a special fund managed by an international board of renowned experts to finance programs

outlined hereunder and compensate the initiator and administrators of this proposal.

6. To establish a $2 trillion Educational Fund to build 50 new universities, with a mission to educate new cadre of global leaders, promote peace, cultural diversity, tolerance, critical thinking, creativity, and innovation, and develop environmentally friendly technologies; all universities would be strategically located to serve most regions of the world.
7. To establish a $2 trillion Humanitarian Fund to help victims of war and natural disasters such as hurricanes, tsunamis, earthquakes, serious diseases, and refugees worldwide.
8. To establish a $2 trillion Environmental Fund to restore the global environment to its past glory with its blue skies, rivers, and seas, and to preserve forests, rare plants, and animals.
9. To establish a $6 trillion Sustainable Development Fund to assist developing nations transform their traditional cultures, grow their economies, reduce poverty, create millions of jobs for the unemployed, and join the industrial world.

The moment a nation pays its debt and management fees as outlined above, it becomes free of debt, and the IMF assumes responsibility for its debt obligations. Since a global economy needs a global central bank to function properly, the new role assigned to the IMF and the issuance of the Ramo would serve to restructure the international monetary system, basing it on a "new gold standard." Since the IMF does not have enough gold, a golden Ramo, backed by the good faith and currencies and economies of all member states would become the international standard against which all other currencies would be pegged, making all currencies more stable and less susceptible to manipulation. Exporters of oil, natural gas, and strategic commodities would be able to price their exports in Ramos, enabling them to forecast future incomes more accurately. Meanwhile, using the Ramo to price the major export commodities will guarantee fairness; no nation would pay less as the value of its currency appreciates against the dollar; no nation would pay more as its currency depreciates against the dollar. The issuance of the Ramo will mark a new era in our history in which the international community of nations will have finally acknowledged that all economies have become, not just interdependent, but largely integrated.

Since budget deficits include interest payments to service the debt, many states would see their deficits vastly reduced the moment they pay their debt. Many states are likely to see their deficits disappear overnight. Such a development would calm global financial anxiety, restore investor and consumer confidence, strengthen banks, and give all states a decade or so to restructure their spending and tax policies to balance their annual budgets.

Concerns and Fear of Inflation

Some economists will most likely argue that repaying the debt in this fashion amounts to printing money and issuing credit notes not backed by solid assets like gold and silver. This is true, but so is the printing of Dollars, Euros, Pounds, and other currencies; these are currencies backed by the good faith of the states issuing them, not by gold or other assets. Compared to these currencies, the Ramo will be backed, not only by one state but by all IMF member states. Furthermore, if the debt is not paid now as proposed, any debt repayment in the future will be made in dollars or Euros or another currency; in fact, all loans are made and repaid in regular currencies that lack material backing. Therefore, the means to pay today as well as later are the same; the only difference is to pay today, free all nations from the debt burden, revitalize the world economy, help the poor or wait until some states default, and cause the banking and credit and trading systems to stop functioning.

Other economists might argue that creating that much money would ignite inflation and hurt consumers everywhere. This is simply incorrect. The IMF has no mandate to spend a penny of the money it will receive except as outlined above. The proposed arrangement for debt repayment changes the identity of the payer only, not the amount to be paid or when to be paid. Though the IMF is required to pay debt notes as they become due on behalf of its member states, it could arrange, in coordination with concerned beneficiaries, to delay some payments and keep the money for as long as needed to maintain financial stability.

On the other hand, helping poor nations develop their economies and transform their cultures is expected to create millions of investment opportunities annually for decades to come; the Sustainable Development Fund, to be outlined in the next section, will facilitate the creation of millions of jobs in the developed and developing countries alike. Moreover, as the IMF pays back loans, it should give lenders the option of getting paid in the same currencies of the loans or in Ramos. This action will limit the increase in the supply of all national currencies while paving the way for the Ramo to play its intended international role as a global reserve currency.

In addition, the Ramo plan is also a plan to deal with the threat of inflation; it provides all developing states with the capital, knowledge, and technical assistance they need to develop their economies, improve labor productivity and food security, transform their cultures, and strengthen business ethics. Nonetheless, no plan can guarantee that inflationary pressures, corruption, or greed will disappear any time soon; the issue of moral hazard will stay with us for as long as we live. No rich or poor, developed or developing nation is immune to it.

The issuance of the Ramo and the arrangements to pay all nations' debt remove all risks associated with possible state defaults and bank failures. Meanwhile, the establishment of the Sustainable Development Fund, the Educational, the Humanitarian, and the Sustainable Environmental funds have the potential to double international trade in a few years and stimulate all economies; it will also create millions of new investment opportunities and tens of millions of new jobs worldwide.

In fact, paying the global debt in its entirety would save all nations about $4 trillion annually in interest payments; the developed countries' share of this savings is about $1 trillion because they pay lower interest rates than developing countries. Today, the service sector employs millions of people in the United States, Europe, and other countries like India without investing almost any money in creating those jobs. People working from their homes and using their own computers are making sales by promoting products and bank services, making resort and travel reservations, helping people fix computer problems, and more. Nevertheless, assuming that creating each job in a poor country needs $10,000 because such jobs would be a mixture of agricultural, industrial, and service jobs, each $1 trillion in interest savings would create about 100 million jobs.

Sustainable Development Fund

As explained earlier, the rapid economic development of several Asian states has caused the industrial production capacity of the world economies to surpass its absorption capacity, creating a wide gap between the global supply of and the global demand for most industrial products.

Without expanding global markets to narrow this gap, the average rate of the world's economic growth will decline further, and the world community of nations will fail to address the economic, financial, and social challenges it faces. Such challenges include how to end regional wars and ease the political turmoil in many parts of the world, and how to deal with the roots of radicalism, terrorism, and human trafficking. Without growing the economies of developing nations and making the global economy fair, it will be even harder to produce enough food to feed the increasing numbers of the poor in Africa, Asia, and Latin America, create jobs for the unemployed, and ease economic and conflict migrations from poor countries plagued by poverty and conflict to Western societies.

For example, the World Bank, after 75 years of working in the development field and spending billions of dollars each year, has failed to help one country develop and industrialize; and this, in turn, has caused almost all theories of economic development written between the 1950s and 1980s to be abandoned. Consequently, new books on development have begun to focus on issues of development such as freedom, corruption, poverty, inequality, education, environmental protection, and women empowerment. There is no doubt that these issues are important; they affect the lives of people and the direction of development and its chances of success; however, these issues are manifestations of deeper sociocultural problems, and therefore cannot be addressed separately.

If helping poor nations was a luxury in the near past, it is a global security and human necessity today. Global Political stability cannot be restored, and radicalism cannot be contained without economic growth and a fairer distribution of wealth and income among social classes and nations. Economic aid and charity cannot create enough jobs for the unemployed to undermine radicalism or increase global demand for goods and services. Since our world has become a global village, no nation can live in peace for long unless other nations feel at least financially comfortable and politically stable; and no nation will feel secure unless its neighbors feel secure as well.

The spread of poverty in many parts of the world, coupled with rising awareness of the living conditions on the other side of the global economic and cultural divides, have created groups of angry, often alienated, and radicalized young people in several parts of the world, particularly in the Middle East and Africa; those people feel betrayed by their leaders and the West. Because their grievances continue to be ignored, their anger rises as their numbers grow and their targets spread.

Since these groups grew out of frustration and despair, the idea to change the world according to their beliefs has become an ideology that motivates them to act, often on their own. So, as long as the current sociopolitical and socioeconomic conditions continue, the radicalization of young people will continue, and so will the killing of people, and the destruction of cities and mankind's historical treasures.

Despite the remarkable increase in China's and India's industrial capacity, both states still have millions of people without work. Every new industrial job created in those countries will aggravate the imbalance between the global supply and the global demand for manufactured goods and technical services. Failure to acknowledge this fact and act accordingly will intensify global competition, raise the level of tension between states, and heighten the vulnerability of the global economy to recurring recessions and financial crises; it will also worsen trade imbalances, increase budget deficits and public debts, and deepen sociocultural and sociopolitical problems in most countries.

As mentioned earlier, it is believed that the size of the global debt is about $120 trillion. The 10% management fees would generate $12 trillion; $6 trillion would be used to launch the educational, humanitarian, and environmental funds, and $6 trillion to launch the Sustainable Development Fund (SDF). A special societal development plan would be developed by the World Bank and other national and international agencies for each country, and money would be spent over 20–25 years to purchase whatever is needed to launch national development plans to restructure the national economies and transform the sociocultural aspects of life in society. The following goals define the mission of SDF:

1. Helping the developing and underdeveloped nations build modern roads, ports, railroads, airports, bridges and dams, electrical grids, water and sewage systems, and basic industries.
2. Modernizing agricultural farming machinery and techniques, improving irrigation systems, train farmers and farmworkers, develop rural communities, revive traditional industries, and upgrade financial management systems,
3. Helping civil society organizations grow in size and effectiveness, and empower the courts to fight corruption, enforce the rule of law, and protect people's rights and the environment.
4. Building enough schools, universities, hospitals, and clinics, train schoolteachers, physicians, nurses, engineers, and technicians to

meet the educational and healthcare needs of growing urban and rural populations.

5. Designing special training programs for workers to acquire the right skills and attitudes to perform efficiently; all workers should be taught how to appreciate time, work, and money to keep the economy growing, and state institutions functioning properly.
6. Supporting national universities and technical schools, and fund research institutes committed to identifying local and national problems and finding homegrown solutions sensitive to traditional customs and values and belief systems.
7. Raising public awareness of the importance of changing attitudes toward science, work, time, life, and the environment, and improving the quality of education and healthcare.
8. Facilitating the creation of a fairly large middle class aware of its social role, and training a new, professionally qualified, and socially responsible entrepreneurial and managerial class.
9. Strengthening food security and energy supply chains at the national and regional levels; and
10. Launching a genuine sociocultural transformation process in each country, according to its needs in the present and prospects in the future.

Two points need to be emphasized: first, all educational and healthcare systems in the Third World lack efficient management systems; second, most members of existing business class in poor and rich countries tend to be corrupt and lack social responsibility. Therefore, the creation of a new ethical entrepreneurial class is a must; otherwise, a lot of money will be wasted, and SDF will not be able to fulfill its entire mission.

Educational Fund

As people of the world get more and more connected forming a global village, the leadership of this village has proven to be neither qualified nor ready to lead collectively and ensure the protection of the environment and the safety of people. I believe that our world has never had a collective leadership that is so politically and economically corrupt, and morally and intellectually bankrupt. The educational fund is intended to train future leaders to manage our global village. Though our world has become one large, highly diversified community, our village lacks a leadership committed to the general welfare of the village's inhabitants. What we have today is a largely narrow-minded leadership that thinks small and works to divide rather than unite the world peoples, to dehumanize some and glorify others rather than humanize everyone and dehumanize no one. So to stay on the top, our leaders have become tribal leaders who incite the people to fight and kill each other, and destroy our environment, heritage, and chances for peace, stability, and progress.

Students attending the Global University system, which plans to have 50 campuses, would be chosen on the bases of their grades and aptitude tests, and the fund would pay for their education. To enable students to gain a global outlook and learn about other cultures and peoples through living, all students would be required to spend their college life at two or more campuses. Universities would try to have equal numbers of undergraduate and graduate students, as well as males and females. While undergraduate programs concentrate on educating students to be global citizens committed to peace, equal opportunity, social justice, environmental sustainability, cultural and religious diversity, and tolerance; graduate programs would concentrate on research in all technical and social fields, with emphasis on developing innovations to make our lives enjoyable, our global economy and environment sustainable, our world peaceful, and our village more livable and loveable.

As the educational fund works to recruit the smartest students available, it will try to design study programs that meet the current and future needs of the peoples of the world. There is no doubt that there are many great universities in the United States, Western Europe, and Asia that continue to lead in technical innovations and research in humanities and social sciences; however, the work of Western universities has largely been dedicated to serving the needs of industrial countries and societies, and the world's largest corporations. As a result, the less developed countries have become dependent on educational systems and programs that lack the capacity to understand the poor nations' cultures and deal with their socioeconomic and sociocultural needs that differ from those of the industrial and knowledge societies.

In the summer of 1991, I was invited by the Swedish government to participate in the "European Conversations" conference. The invitation signed by Mr. Odd Engström, then deputy prime minister, included the following paragraph: "I would like to arrange a meeting between leading thinkers and thinking leaders to discuss how we are to succeed in reconciling political legitimacy and economic rationality in a Europe where national borders have lost more of their significance. Can we establish democracy at a new, regional level? How can the new Europe create welfare for so many? Is there a common identity that embraces all this multiplicity of mutually intertwined national destinies – and, if so, is this something we want?".

The number of participants in the conference was about 30 persons, 18 were invited from outside Sweden; the British economist Amartya Sen and I were among this group of participants. On the second day of our discussion, Sen asked me a question; believing that I might be able to answer; he said: "I have a puzzling, largely troubling question for which I have no answer: Can you tell me why most people in the Third World lie? After giving that question some thought, I found the question quite simple. I told my colleagues that day that most people of the Third World lie because they lack freedom. When young men and women have no social freedom, every time they do something that violates traditional customs, they lie to their parents; when people have no religious freedom, every time they ignore a religious duty they lie to everyone who takes religious rituals seriously; when intellectuals have no freedom of speech, every time they are asked about their views and opinions they lie in public and to the police; when investors have no economic freedom, every time they violate established laws they lie to the government. So, lack of social, religious, political, and economic freedoms, as well as freedom of speech is the major force that motivates, at times compels most Third World people to lie.

And when lying becomes an acceptable habit that seldom finds anyone to challenge, social, political, economic, and religious corruption spreads and deepens its roots in society. Consequently, trust and honesty disappear, social responsibility crumbles, business ethics vanish, and prospects of societal development become very slim. Therefore, no one should expect economic development to succeed in a society that lacks freedom, particularly, political, social, and religious freedom. Development requires two basic changes to succeed: economic restructuring and sociocultural transformation; however, sociocultural transformation is not possible without modernizing and humanizing the educational system.[5] In 1998, Amartya Sen was awarded the Nobel Memorial Prize in Economics, and in 1999, he published his widely recognized book, "Development as Freedom."

As a graduate student in the late 1960s, I argued that the "economic development" concept was misconceived from the beginning. Assuming that economic development in an underdeveloped state is possible without developing the human resources, cultures, institutions, and the politics of that nation. This assumption amounts to treating the economy and society as two separate facets of life; thus ignoring the fact that no economy can function without people, and no people can survive without a productive economy. The failure of development thinking in the West to identify the root causes of poverty and underdevelopment in poor countries and articulate feasible approaches to development are largely responsible for wasting trillions of dollars, rare opportunities, and valuable time, while causing billions of people to suffer poverty and indignation for decades needlessly. This means that there is a need for a new approach to dealing with the issues of development and underdevelopment. Development must be treated as a comprehensive societal process; it must be viewed as a bird that needs two healthy wings to fly and navigate the blue skies; with one wing only, the bird might be able to jump and run but it cannot fly. So is development; to succeed and achieve its noble objectives, it needs economic restructuring and sociocultural transformation.

David Landes argues that the major key to wealth is openness, which means openness to new ideas and to borrowing from other nations the technologies that are productive. While openness to new technologies is important to economic development, openness to new ideas is important to political change and sociocultural transformation, and thus to moving society from feudalism and totalitarianism to freedom and justice. Nevertheless, no societal change is possible unless the social, cultural, and religious environments are transformed. To make these environments hospitable to change, we need to first build creative and innovative education systems, have an educated and enlightened class of men and women to manage them, and lead society to societal development.

So developing nations need educational systems that recognize the need to borrow new technologies and learn from the experiences of nations that are more developed. This means that developing nations need to borrow productive technologies and adopt ideas that help them transform their political systems and traditional cultures; no societal change is possible without transforming the social, cultural, and religious environments to be hospitable to change. There is also a need to build innovative educational systems and train enlightened generations of men and women to manage such systems, and this is what the proposed educational fund is supposed to do.

Humanitarian Fund

The humanitarian fund is intended to meet the emergency needs of all peoples affected by natural disasters such as tsunamis, hurricanes, earthquakes, floods, starvation, drought, and epidemics, as well as man-made disasters such as civil wars. War and conflict cause people to suffer and live in miserable conditions as refugees in need of food, medicine, jobs, education, and hope. The humanitarian fund will have its staff and system in place to swiftly deliver assistance wherever it may be needed; it will also have the necessary supplies to respond immediately and comprehensively to all emergencies. The fund will work with similar national and international organizations to meet the urgent needs of suffering people everywhere; it will also act as an accredited UN agency to evaluate and accredit not-for-profit organizations working in the field of international relief and humanitarian assistance.

Dealing with past and present environmental and human catastrophes seems to indicate that no national or international organization has the capacity to deal with large scale property destruction or human dislocation. While Katrina had exposed the limitations and impotence of US government agencies, the 2010 earthquake in Haiti and the 2015 earthquake in Nepal, and the 2011 floods in Pakistan and refugees fleeing gang violence in Latin America and conflict in Africa and the Middle East have proven that neither national nor international organizations have the capacity to provide timely assistance to desperate people in need; in fact, after many years, some needs of the victims of the incidents mentioned above are yet to be met.

If the money of the Humanitarian Fund were to be invested in US government bonds at an annual interest rate of 2.5%, the fund's income would be $50 billion a year; more than enough to meet the challenges of global emergences year after year, probably for eternity. Consequently, the need for donor conferences to raise money for victims of natural disasters and man-made wars and making pledges of help that do not usually get paid in full will be eliminated. Victims' needs would be met without hassle and without using financial aid as a tool to coerce poor states and manipulate poor people, thus the dignity of the poor and weak would be respected, and their needs and rights would be honored.

Sustainable Environmental Fund

Since the 1970s, the world has become progressively more aware of the damage caused to the environment by neglect and misuse; as a result, the need to protect the environment has become a priority in many parts of the world. However, despite the substantive work that has been done in this field, no environmentalist or government agency can say with confidence if we are approaching environmental sustainability or still moving away from it. If the $2 trillion devoted to this fund were to be invested in US government bonds at an annual interest rate of 2.5%, the fund's income would be $50 billion a year, enough to hire about 10,000 scientists, 20,000 engineers, and one million workers to take care of our mother earth and protect our environment from abuse and misuse.

As national agencies strive to achieve sustainable development, they tend to treat sustainability as a domestic rather than global endeavor. But environmental sustainability is unattainable except at the international level because many nations have access to nonrenewable resources like water and natural gas to waste, and rivers and seas to pollute, without giving enough consideration to the interests of other nations that depend on the same resources. Therefore, fairness and reality dictate that sustainability must be treated as a global endeavor, and the sacrifices needed to accomplish it and the benefits generated by it should be shared by all nations.

Since development is a comprehensive societal process, no economic plan can succeed in a traditional society without being preceded or accompanied by a plan to transform the sociocultural aspects of life in society.[6] Economic restructuring, sociocultural transformation, and investment in education, healthcare, and infrastructure, and environmental preservation, which SDF and the other three funds intend to do, would increase women's awareness and free most of them from the chains of ignorance and traditions, and thus empower them to regain self-confidence and become more active workers and respected members of society. This should cause population growth rates to decline gradually, leading the demographics of most developing nations to approach those of the European nations within 10–15 years.

Helicopter Money

Believing that a new recession is coming soon, the Economist said on February 20, 2016, "Policymakers in rich economies need to consider some radical approaches to tackling the next downturn. In considering alternative approaches, the Economist added that; "there is a deeper concern that, if or when that recession comes, policymakers will have very few options for dealing with it."[7] It is clear that the Economist sees no point in repeating what was done before; implying that neither stimulus packages nor austerity measures can deal with the expected recession, especially after central banks had then reduced interest rates to near zero. Consequently, the Economist suggests, though reluctantly, using what economist Milton Friedman called "Helicopter money," which means printing as much money as needed to repay the debt. But following this advice limits the number of states that could wipe out their debt to only a few ones that include the United States, members of the Eurozone, Britain, Switzerland, Japan, and probably China. However, most other nations cannot.

There is no doubt that America can print as much money as needed to repay its debt and more; the US Federal Reserve has been printing money since 2009 without interruption but printing over $32 trillion in weeks or even months cannot be done without consequences. An increase in the money supply of this magnitude is more likely to cause inflation, devalue the dollar, and invite other nations, particularly the Eurozone nations, China, Britain, and Japan to devalue their currencies to remain competitive. Since most other currencies are pegged, in one way or another to the US dollar, attempts to devalue the dollar become pointless. However, such an action would cause world confidence in America's wisdom and leadership to be vastly undermined; and this, in turn, would diminish the attractiveness of the US dollar as the world's premier reserve currency.

Even if the Helicopter option were feasible, is it fair and morally acceptable that a few nations print as much money as they wish to repay their debt and leave billions of people to languish in debt and poverty? Is it fair and morally acceptable that such a group liberates itself from the debt burden when most of the money that the poor nations had borrowed was stolen by dictators and corrupt politicians, and foreign corporations and deposited in American and European banks? The fair and morally acceptable way to repay the debt is to liberate all nations from the debt burden at once; such an action would create a new sense of fraternity among all nations, revitalize the world economy, reduce poverty, and undermine racism and radicalism that often lead to hatred, terrorism, and war.

Is the so-called helicopter money similar to the Ramo plan? And if the two plans differ from each other, how does the Ramo plan differ from the helicopter plan? The Ramo plan is different in several important ways.

1. Helicopter money is a scheme to enable a few countries to print money freely and repay their debt. Since this option is limited to some states, other nations would not be able to liberate themselves from debt. As a result, the poor nations would most likely default, creating more complicated problems for themselves and the rich states.
2. By freeing the rich states of debt while leaving the poor states to pay interest on their debt to rich states, the impoverished peoples would be reduced to mere slaves working to enrich the rich in exchange for more poverty and extra misery. This is more likely to deepen alienation, spread hatred, and increase terrorism. As a consequence, the world would be divided into rich masters and poor slaves; causing every party involved in this sick relationship to lose a good deal of its humanity.
3. An exclusive Helicopter plan for the rich would prevent the implementation of the Ramo plan and the establishment of the educational, humanitarian, environmental, and sustainable development funds. Without these funds, the old economic, sociocultural, and political problems would intensify, causing poverty to increase and resentment in poor states to rise; it will also cause many social ills to become endemic. As a consequence, the flood of economic and war refugees would rise, leading to more internal strife, racism, and fear in Europe and America.
4. Using the Helicopter option to liberate the industrial nations from debt is likely to help the rich countries' economies to grow modestly for a few years only because the limited financial resources available to the world's poor would prevent them from becoming active consumers.
5. Printing trillions of dollars to repay the debt of the richest nations only is likely to disrupt the international monetary system and cause uncertainty. Poor nations that cannot do what the rich ones can, would vehemently oppose such a plan because accepting it means accepting outrageous debt servicing obligations and more

poverty. Moreover, such a plan would poison the international atmosphere and create bitterness that leads to forming new international alliances that seek to undermine the power and interests of the rich nations.

6. If the Helicopter option were to be implemented, the rich nations' actions would be viewed as unfair and imperialistic because no nation should be entitled to indulge in conspicuous consumption for decades and then print money freely to pay for its bad behavior. On the other hand, since taken such action would be unprecedented, it will have serious consequences no one can foresee. One of the more likely consequences is a collective action by the poor nations to default on their foreign debt and stop paying interest to the rich nations and their banks, causing many Western banks to collapse; and this is likely to trigger a global depression lasting a decade or more. A collective default by the poor nations would be fully justified and would be encouraged by the world's leading intellectuals, human rights organizations, and many economists across the globe; and the feeling of bitterness toward the rich nations would last for generations.

Therefore, the full implementation of the Ramo plan is the only viable and fair option to save the world economy and secure a better future for future generations. In addition to freeing all nations from the debt burden, the plan would reduce world population growth rates to probably half of 1% within few years, place the global economy on a sustainable growth path, protect our mother earth, create a new spirit of equality and fraternity among all nations, and vastly weaken the power and rationale of the ideologies of racism, radicalism, and terrorism. Our global village, as a result, would become the place to love and enjoy living in. It will also make the plan's achievements a shared human experience to be remembered and cherished forever.

Notes

1. Rabie, *Global Economic and Cultural Transformation*, Palgrave Macmillan, 2013, 167–174.
2. Vitor Gaspar, Paulo Medas, and Roberto Perrelli, Private Debt Reaches a Record $226 Trillion, https://blogs.imf.org/2021/12/15/global-debt-reaches-a-record-226-trillion/.

3. Trading Economics; Country List of Government Debt to GDP, https://tradingeconomics.com/country-list/government-debt-to-gdp.
4. Brian Chappatta, $250 Trillion in Debt: The World's Post-Lehman Legacy, Bloomberg, September. 13, 2018, https://www.bloomberg.com/graphics/2018-lehman-debt/.
5. Ibid., Rabie; *A Theory of Sustainable Sociocultural and Economic Development*, Palgrave Macmillan, 2016, Chapter 11.
6. Ibid., Rabie, *A Theory of Sustainable Sociocultural and Economic Development*, Chapter 3.
7. Fighting the next recession: unfamiliar ways forward, the Economist, February 20, 2016.

CHAPTER 16

Concluding Remarks

Abstract In every society, the fortunes of each person are a function of his ability to recognize the opportunities open to him and exploit them without delay. In industrial society in particular, income and the means to earn a good income have become the major forces separating one class from the other. However, as the knowledge age advances, the requirements to recognize and exploit opportunities have become complex; they need capital, skills, experience, and formal and informal education. As a consequence, the traditional socioeconomic gaps separating the rich and poor began to reflect sociocultural divides. Due to the adoption of the free market philosophy in the 1980s, the middle class began to lose income and power and shrink in size, losing its influence and constructive role in society. The economic shift from manufacturing to services and the changing nature of knowledge itself have caused opportunities open to members of the middle class to narrow drastically and irreversibly. A knowledge barrier, consequently, was added to the capital and skill barriers causing upward mobility in the new economy to decline substantially. This chapter explains what had happened, why it happened, and what is needed to adjust to the new reality and regain what was lost and live a normal life.

Keywords Socioeconomic gaps · Sociocultural divides · Capital and skill barriers · Super-rich · Middle class · Outsourcing · South Korea · Japan ·

M. Rabie, *A Future Economy for All*,
https://doi.org/10.1007/978-3-031-42957-6_16

China · Center of military power · Center of economic power · Peace and Development Foundation · Institute for Creative Ideas

In every society, the fortunes of each member are a function of his ability to recognize the opportunities open to him and exploit them without delay. In industrial society in particular, income and the means to earn a good income are the major forces separating one class from the other. However, as the knowledge age advances, the requirements to recognize and exploit opportunities have become complex, demanding capital, skills, experience, and formal and informal education. As a consequence, the traditional socioeconomic gaps separating the rich and poor began to reflect sociocultural divides. Due to the adoption of the free market philosophy in the 1980s, the middle class began to lose income, power, and opportunity and shrink in size. The economic shift from manufacturing to services and the changing nature of knowledge itself have caused opportunities open to members of the middle class to narrow drastically. A knowledge barrier, consequently, was added to the capital and skill barriers causing upward mobility in the new economy to decline substantially.

Today, most people have become more materialistic and less spiritual and ethical than ever before, giving more attention to making money and less to living meaningful lives. People, particularly members of the rich class and the talented knowledge workers, tend to fight largely on their own to win battles they often frame by themselves. Such people have difficulty accepting reality as it is; they are constantly on the move searching for new realities to shape, new opportunities to exploit, and new virtual relationships to forge. In addition, such people seem to be seeking more pleasure, wealth, and power, while trying to minimize worry, risk, and pain. As a result, a privileged class made up of the super-rich has emerged to control money and power, causing poverty to spread, and the traditional middle class to be squeezed. Out of that squeeze comes a moral crisis that makes most people want to cut loose from those who are suffering.

In the meantime, as profits generated by overseas operations increase and foreign markets expand, national corporations' dependence on domestic markets and workers diminishes. And as national workers become less competitive due to higher wages and social benefits or due to changing production technologies, national companies seek cheaper labor and investment opportunities in foreign markets. But by outsourcing and moving operations overseas, unemployment at home rises, wages and benefits decline, and the national economy slows down or stagnates; and this undermines the capacity of the national economy to create the kind of jobs required to support a solid middle class. Moreover, as industrial and knowledge jobs migrate to countries like China and South Korea, research and development institutions migrate with them. "This is why the patent applications from the Asian nations of China, India, Japan, and South Korea surpassed those of the United States and all other Western nations in 2008".[1] In fact, while the center of military power is still in the West, the center of economic power is shifting fast from the West to the East.

Individualism and a strong desire to compete and succeed have become the major forces driving the rich and knowledge workers in this age. People managing investment banks, mutual funds, mortgage, and insurance companies have become creatures of the moment; always on the move searching for short-term profits and fast deals to make. Even before the financial crisis of 2008. The financial products which banks invented and marketed were not meant to create new jobs or national wealth; instead, they were meant to create personal wealth for managers of large banks and hedge funds and financial traders. As a consequence, financial products created a small number of jobs, while causing the concentrating of most wealth in fewer hands, denying most members of the middle class and the poor the financial means they needed to be active consumers and live decent lives.

An equitable distribution of income and wealth is the only way to creating more demand and a better world for all. Nevertheless, an equitable distribution of income and wealth does not guarantee a stronger, more active middle class, or lead to a healthier, more competitive economy. More money in the hands of people will encourage them to spend more; but does not compel them to invest or produce more. Thus a policy to enable employees to become shareholders and encourage them to build equity in the companies they work for is the only feasible way to put them on the right path to middle-class status. That would lead them to become aware of their interests and appreciate the benefits of saving and investing; it will also narrow the wealth and income gaps in society. I believe that paying employees 25% of their salaries in shares of corporations they work for and deal with should become a golden universal rule;

otherwise, no middle class anywhere in the world would be sustained for long; and no corporation will be socially responsible or loyal to a nation or humanity.

The money suggested to reward the initiator and administrators of the Ramo plan would be added to the money allocated to reward the initiator and administrators of the MoRa plan. So half of one percent of the money created to finance the Ramo programs would go to foster the capabilities of the "Peace and Development Foundation" (PDF), and the "Institute for Creative Ideas" (ICI); ICI would guide the work of PDF, which aims to promote peace and sociocultural transformation; grow the local and regional capacities to solve conflict peacefully; empower the poor and weak, with emphasis on women; discover and develop young people's talents; fight homelessness and poverty; and train young people how to think critically and rationally and stay away from violence, drugs, and radicalism; it will also be used to encourage reading in order to eliminate cultural illiteracy in the less developed countries. However, it is suggested that Prof. Rabie gets one half of 1% of this money to further promote his ideas worldwide, help people who need help but cannot be helped through the Foundation for Development and Peace.

Prof. Rabie would like to be able to help every person who played a role in his life and career, students who forced him to consider issues he did think of before, classmates who have become grand grandparents but still living in refugee camps, young men and women he encountered as he taught and lectured in about 50 countries and more than 400 universities and conferences worldwide; young people who challenged and humbled him by their foresight and courage.

Note

1. Rabie, Saving Capitalism and Democracy, 136.

Index

M. Rabie, *A Future Economy for All*,
https://doi.org/10.1007/978-3-031-42957-6

SPRINGER NATURE

GPSR Compliance

The European Union's (EU) General Product Safety Regulation (GPSR) is a set of rules that requires consumer products to be safe and our obligations to ensure this.

If you have any concerns about our products, you can contact us on ProductSafety@springernature.com

In case Publisher is established outside the EU, the EU authorized representative is:

Springer Nature Customer Service Center GmbH
Europaplatz 3
69115 Heidelberg, Germany

Kolibri 360 GmbH
Ferdinand-Jühlke-Straße 7
99095 Erfurt, Deutschland
produktsicherheit@kolibri360.de